Discussion at Bellagio

Discussion

~~~~~~~~~~~~~~~~~~~~~~~~~~~~~

Compiled and Edited by K. H. SILVERT

with

David E. Apter	Charles F. Gallagher
Giorgio Borsa	Alan W. Horton
E. A. Bayne	Yusuf Ibish
Des Alwi	Yoichi Itagaki
James Eayrs	Ali Mazrui
Khodadad Farmanfarmaian	Laurence I. Radway
	Leonard Reissman
Juan Gómez Millas	Dennison I. Rusinow

at Bellagio

THE POLITICAL ALTER-
NATIVES *of* DEVELOPMENT

ഗഗഗഗഗഗഗഗഗഗഗഗ

A Conference on *The Nation and The Political Alternatives of Development,* under auspices of the American Universities Field Staff and held at Villa Serbelloni, Bellagio, Italy, March 8–20, 1964

AMERICAN UNIVERSITIES FIELD STAFF, INC.
366 Madison Avenue,   New York, N.Y. 10017

THE NATION AND THE POLITICAL ALTERNATIVES
OF DEVELOPMENT

A conference under auspices of the American Universities Field Staff
held at
The Rockefeller Foundation Villa Serbelloni, Bellagio, Italy
March 8–20, 1964

IN ATTENDANCE

DAVID E. APTER
Professor of Political Science
University of California
  at Berkeley

GIORGIO BORSA
Professor of Modern History
University of Pavia, Milan

E. A. BAYNE
Staff Associate, AUFS
(Iran, Italy, Israel, Somalia)

DES ALWI
Former Indonesian Public Serv-
  ant, now Businessman, Kuala
  Lumpur, Malaysia

JAMES EAYRS
Professor of Political Economy
University of Toronto
Canada

KHODADAD FARMANFARMAIAN
Deputy Governor, The Central
  Bank of Iran

JUAN GÓMEZ MILLAS
Retired, former Rector
University of Chile

CHARLES F. GALLAGHER
Staff Associate, AUFS
(The Arab World)

TEG C. GRONDAHL
Executive Director, AUFS

ALAN W. HORTON
Staff Associate, AUFS
(United Arab Republic)

YUSUF IBISH
Professor of Political Science
American University of Beirut

YOICHI ITAGAKI
Professor of International
  Relations
Hitotsubashi University
Tokyo, Japan

ALI MAZRUI
Professor of Political Science
Makerere University College
Uganda

LAURENCE I. RADWAY
Professor of Government
Dartmouth College
Hanover, N.H.

LEONARD REISSMAN
Professor of Sociology
Tulane University
New Orleans, Louisiana

DENNISON I. RUSINOW
Staff Associate, AUFS
(Yugoslavia)

K. H. SILVERT
Director of Studies, AUFS

Professional Assistant:
  Magalí Sarfatti
  Ecole Pratique des Hautes
    Etudes
  Paris

(Note: No extensive biographies are given, for each participant provides
his own intellectual identification in the course of the conversations
recorded in this report.)

Preface

This book came out of the first international meeting to be sponsored by The American Universities Field Staff. Although the title page identifies Mr. Silvert as compiler and editor, *Discussion at Bellagio* has had as much authorship as editorship from him. It is not a symposium, nor a verbatim playback, nor just an edited report; rather it is a book inspired by a conference on The Nation and the Political Alternatives of Development. It re-creates two weeks of always articulate, often crackling, frequently brilliant, but never acrimonious, exchanges.

The meeting did not set out to arrive at a list of agreed conclusions and Mr. Silvert has not tried to present a consensus. Nevertheless, he has been faithful to the sources of his inspiration. The essence of the conference is reported lucidly and the contributions, whether oral, written, or both, are given full scope. The author has caught the participants in their most glowing moments. Reconstructing their oral presentations, he has, I suspect, now and then given a leg up to put a discussant firmly astride Pegasus.

The book centers on Mr. Silvert's intellectual and professional response to the impressive array of information, ideas, and theories put forward during the discussions; and throughout he cogently argues his own position. He believes that comparative but still detailed operational theories of nationalism and development can be stated and tested, and that there probably are relationships between nationalism and development and between freedom and development of great importance both to scholars and policymakers.

Not explicit in *Discussion at Bellagio* is the importance of the part played by Mr. Silvert. It was he who drafted the agenda; who, enjoying almost total recall and an extraordinary facility for synthesis, was often called upon to recapitulate and refocus the discussion; who plumped for generalization and theoretical application when the range of the data or the lure of the particular threatened to displace discussion with conversation.

It is gratifying to the American Universities Field Staff that its first international conference should have been so well applauded by the participants. (One said that out of the variety of knowledge and disciplinary approaches brought to bear in the sessions he had gained the equivalent of three years of intensive reading.) The AUFS is deeply grateful for the quality of thinking and the diversity of knowledge its guests brought to the conference table. In this book Mr. Silvert has made clear the advantages of the conference to the AUFS, as it moves on with comparative studies while continuing its program of foreign area research and reporting.

By publishing the report as a book the AUFS hopes to extend the usefulness of an unusually productive meeting. Students, social scientists, policymakers, and readers in general will find much in it that is pertinent to a major problem of this decade: how to cope with the process of social, economic, and political development.

New York   Teg C. Grondahl, Executive Director
August 3, 1964   American Universities Field Staff

Contents

Introduction

The idea of a conference on some aspect of the politics of development and the growth of nationalism germinated in the warmth of a dinner in Hanover, New Hampshire, in early 1963. Little more than a year separated this early notion and the preparation of this final report. Several choices made very early determined the tone and style of the meeting, as well as its subject matter. The overarching decision was that the conference was to concern primarily the *politics* of developing countries, with economic, social, religious, cultural, and other aspects of social change to enter into the discussions only as they directly pertained to matters of public policy and power. We also decided on a small group of perhaps fifteen or sixteen persons and on a meeting period of two weeks in order to give everyone unhurried time to stretch his ideas as he might wish.

To achieve the spontaneity and unvarnished personal interplay allowed by the time and the smallness of the group, we also determined to ask for no prepared papers. Formal presentations, a requisite for short meetings, tend to freeze individuals into defensive postures. We felt that a wide-ranging and, if possible, virtuosic treatment of political development was highly desirable for a subject which is still fresh and somewhat amorphous, still on the frontier of social science knowledge.

Economic development has been in fashion for well over a generation as a conference subject. In the mid-1950s social development assumed fascination, especially in the beginning to explain "impediments to economic development," as it was so often put in agendas. But political modernization, perhaps because it is a sensitive subject of little appeal to such meeting-sponsoring organs as the international agencies, has been relatively neglected except among political scientists themselves.

Even though the discipline of political science has only recently turned its concentrated attention on the emergent world, much excellent work has already been published and an invigorating spirit of adventure in this area pervades the field. Our subject, then, had the double advantage of not being routine, but yet of having a literature on which to draw for theories and cases. We hoped to honor this kind of theme with an open format and, most important, sought to guarantee a complicated mosaic of ideas and temperaments by bringing persons from the developing lands together with Europeans and North Americans and making certain that each participant had a fundamental political cast to his interests no matter what his academic field or occupation.

The meeting included six persons from the developing countries and a Canadian, an Italian, and eight Americans—five of them from the American Universities Field Staff and three from United States universities. Seven of the group were professional political scientists, three were political historians, two were economists, one was a sociologist and another an anthropologist, and the list was completed with a practicing revolutionary and an editor-executive. The countries in which these men had done research could be counted literally in the dozens: for example, Ghana, Nigeria, Uganda, Somalia, Morocco, Tunisia, Algeria, Egypt, Lebanon, Israel, Iran, Syria, Indonesia, India, Pakistan, China, Mexico, Guatemala, Chile, Argentina, and even Italy, Japan, the United States, and Canada.

The Rockefeller Foundation generously opened to us its Villa Serbelloni in Bellagio, Italy, and provided the necessary travel and other expenses. Mr. and Mrs. John Marshall, solicitous hosts and skilled directors of the Villa, knew exactly how to blend order and freedom. To them and to the Messrs. Gerald Freund and Kenneth Thompson of the Rockefeller Foundation, we extend our gratitude for their courtesies and our respect for their professionalism. We are indebted also to Miss Magalí Sarfatti for her excellent transcript of the proceedings.

This conference report has no great pretensions. Committees prohibit the personal loneliness from which emerge works of art or grand social theories. But a well-chosen group working articulately and intensively—each in his own way lighting a part of the subject—can together illuminate broad and sometimes richly textured themes. We promised no more than a dry resume of the proceedings to our guests at the conference. But after consideration we decided to attempt a re-creation of the atmosphere and the sense of the meetings, for certainly many ideas, insights, and potential research hypotheses were recorded. What is being attempted here is not a verbatim account, then, but rather a report which, in many places different from the actually spoken words, still reconstructs the meaning and the quality of the meeting as experienced by those at the table.

The participants sometimes jotted down their ideas in rough form. These notes have been reproduced inside quotation marks in the text. Otherwise the version is the responsibility of the editor of this report. Because these paraphrased attributions have not been sent to each conferee for checking, the editor must assume full responsibility for any errors of fact or interpretation in those sections outside of quotation marks.

We are aware that conference reports seldom give the reader the same sense of intellectual soaring experienced by the participants. We also know that most conferences follow the same route—a period of feeling out, a period of staking out firm positions, a period of partial reconciliation and farewell. We decided to run whatever risks may be inherent in this project of reporting, however, in the belief that the reader as active kibitzer may enjoy the play element and find some suggestive ideas. The professional may at least vicariously learn something of his far-flung colleagues, the student may see what his professional mentors do in their meetings, and perhaps other conferences on related subjects may, by turning to this report, find ways to shorten their time of initial sparring.

On the last morning of the meeting our colleagues went early to the conference room and filled a blackboard with good-bys in a score of languages. This manifestation of high youthful spirits also reflected the strong affection which had grown up among us. In return, we in the AUFS hope that this report of their doings will be pleasing to our guests and useful to those concerned with human development.

K. H. S.

CHAPTER ONE

Finding Common Ground

A. *A Theory of the Nation.* The relationship between the nation, nationalism, and political development. The definition of terms: nation, nationalism; economic, social, and political development; democracy, authoritarianism, and so forth, as the participants themselves determine. *Chairman: K. H. Silvert.*

B. *A Theory of the Nation, Continued.* Classical and stereotypical theories of the nation and social change. The Liberal, Hegelian, Marxist, Catholic, and other conceptions of the state and nation. Contemporary ideologies of nationalism and their manifestation in internal dynamics of change as well as in international affairs. Are typologies of nationalistic ideology possible, as measured against given sets of sociopolitical circumstances? *Chairman: Juan Gómez Millas.*

C. *A Theory of the Nation, Concluded.* An appraisal of the Western experience. What is its "reality" for the developed nations and for the emergent states? What can be abstracted from this experience for more general application to the developing world, and what is unique to time and place or to each specific cultural entity? Is there such a thing as "historical periods" which might be useful in prediction and in deciding on levels of theoretical generality? *Chairman: Leonard Reissman.*

I. A THEORY OF THE NATION

A rubble of questioned definitions, uncertainties of conception, and problems of theory, comparative techniques, and method faced the conference after the introductory sessions. But the magic cement of respectful and friendly identification had by then somehow materialized. In the hackneyed phrase, the participants had agreed to disagree. More important, however, means had been found to recast old biases and to test notions, ideas, and full-blown ideological systems against the judgments of the group. The complexities of the subject matter easily mingled with the matured perspectives of the participants to produce a constant swirl of changing agreements and disagreements. No firm blocs formed; skirmishes did not harden into campaigns; even into the last session no "winners" or "losers" emerged. Although design contributed to this happy result, accident must also be praised.

The formal meetings took place around a large table covered with mauve brocade. Everyone had elbow room for stretching and scratching, but all voices were easily heard. We usually met twice a day, but several afternoons as well as the weekend were left free, and the sessions were unequal in length. *Espresso* coffee brought to the table broke the morning sessions, and tea in the afternoon permitted a bit of milling around. Our hosts of the Villa Serbelloni managed matters so as to permit a wide range of informal as well as formal activity. A high correlation exists between the life of the mind and the life of the stomach; food could be both eaten and discussed with interest. The radio-phonograph equipment was excellent, as was the record collection, and intensively used. Through the use of these items, as well as walks and a scattering to Switzerland and many points in northern Italy over the free weekend, the constant interchange among the guests, the continuous knotting and unknotting of relationships, created the air of confidence and social well-being which made the formal discussions flow with the conviction of faith in the good will of one's fellow voyagers. A microcosm of academic freedom thus appeared through an amalgam of personality and ambiance in the creation of mutual respect—the ultimate in the social security of the intellectual. The most necessary and sufficient accident, then, was the fortunate combination of persons who, despite their cultural and intellectual differences, could take pleasure in the interplay of minds about a subject of interest to all of us.

The participants prepared no papers before the meetings. Instead, to stake out a common ground to start the discussions, we sent everyone a copy of *Expectant Peoples: Nationalism and Development,* a comparative study prepared by associates of the AUFS under the editorship of Mr. K. H. Silvert, who, in consequence, assumed responsibility for chairing the first day of sessions. The group asked him to give a summary of the theoretical underpinnings and the conclusions to *Expectant Peoples,* which he did at various times during the first two days.

Expectant Peoples argues that the nation-state is the necessary site within which economic and social modernization takes place and that, therefore, national identification as a social value and the institution of the nation-state together define political development. This construction is controversial for many reasons. Historians use the word "nationalism" in many different senses. Worse, the term has negative connotations in most of the developed world but very positive ones in the developing societies. Sometimes used to refer to ideology, sometimes to sovereignty and nationality, and at other times to a kind of inflated patriotism, nationalism is everybody's doxy and nobody's faithful mistress.

The AUFS study took account of these juridical, symbolic, and ideological definitions of nationalism and added a fourth, "nationalism as social value, that norm defining the loyalty due to fellow citizens and to the mandates of the state, the tacit consent extended to the activities of the state within the national society, and the internalized 'feeling' of national community." The reduction of these four elements led us to suggest that "Nationalism is the acceptance of the state as the impersonal and ultimate arbiter of human affairs." The pertinent explanatory paragraph from the book is:

This statement at first blush must certainly appear overly simple, and perhaps totalitarian in suggestion. What we are pointing out, however, is the core of nationalism: the establishment of a fully secular area of life regulated by a social institution before which all men are at least in certain public senses equal. This aspect of the nation-state is what makes national systems unique, what differentiates them from all other societies. . . . The statement describes a function—the settlement of dispute. It names the state as the institutionalized means of bringing power to bear to satisfy that function. The necessity for the loyal participation of a citizenry within an explicit community which creates the consensual power necessary to the primary function of the state is indicated in the word "acceptance." And the definition states that the function must be exercised "impersonally"—over an appreciable territorial expansion and across broad class lines, in ultimate cases overriding primary loyalties to intermediate family, religious, or other competing areas of identification. Nationality, patriotism, ideology, and social values all may be reflective of this national situation, of this willingness to permit a political institution to settle certain kinds of dispute, and to accept the settlements as though they were ultimate—that is, until such time as they may be changed *within* the polity itself, without institutional break. [P. 19.]

Silvert then related this concept of nationalism to the approaches to development taken by disciplines other than political science. Economic development must imply more than industrialization and increased consumption levels. The mobilization and recruitment of labor and the ordering of market situations call for political functions of an impersonal nature unless economic inefficiency is to result. If kinship is permitted to be a criterion of labor choice, then the development process must suffer because the most capable will not necessarily find appropriate employment. Government, then, is involved in economic development in a primary, systemic way as well as in the administration of capital flow, utilities regulation, and so forth.

Social development, using the same institutional approach, is seen not merely as literacy, extended communications systems, or number of shod feet, but also as a matter of stratification and social class. The function of the nation-state in social development is the creation of a political market place in which all men can be equal for certain purposes. This political market provides equality before the laws for not only moral reasons but also in order to blur class differences and create a sense of community that overrides other divisions. The utility of this device is that it opens a way for persons to escape from socially defined niches into positions somewhat in accord with individual ability. This freeing of individuals from the bonds of ascription (such as family position) into the measures of merit (such as ability unleashed by training) obviously has positive consequences in promoting economic as well as social development. Opening such perspectives for individuals is the immediate product, however, of political development—of a national community equipped with its requisite instruments for the ordering of adjustment between the individual and his modern or modernizing society.

Silvert ended this disquisition by pointing out that, were he now to be writing the introduction to *Expectant Peoples,* he would put much more emphasis on the *quality* of each nation's polity. The book states that national identification is a necessary but insufficient condition both for modern totalitarianism and for democracy. Silvert would now argue that a nation-state must build into its mechanisms certain open and pragmatic procedures if it is to institutionalize change. This subject need not be pursued at this point, for in the conference the matter was left to dangle and was returned to only in the last set of discussions.

No one should imagine, however, that *Expectant Peoples* was accepted as a base line without discussion. Objections ranged from a flat, "That's no theory," to protests that the word "nationalism" itself was ill-chosen. Mr. Giorgio Borsa, for example, noted:

"I feel that the area of disagreement between us is getting narrower and narrower. I will try to define it. It is now mostly a question of words and terminology; I accept your concept, with all its implications. I object to the use of the word nationalism to express it because to me there is an historical meaning attached to it that prevents its being used in the sense you do, without creating confusion. I am thinking of nineteenth-century European nationalism. This cannot be divorced from the concept of nation, from which it sprang. You define nationalism as 'the acceptance of the state as the ultimate arbiter of human affairs.' The European nineteenth-century nationalist would have been horrified at being called a nationalist on those grounds. In fact a nineteenth-century nationalist was a man who did *not* accept the state as such as the ultimate arbiter of human affairs, because the state to him was a purely juridical concept and in itself had no ethical value and could not command his loyalty. It could do so the moment it became identified with a nation, because from being so identified with the nation it acquired an ethical value. (See Fichte's speeches to the German nation.)

"If your concept of nationalism were to be applied to nineteenth-century nationalism, there would have been no nationalist movement at all. Italian or German nineteenth-century nationalists were citizens of one or the other Italian or German state. If their being nationalists should have consisted in 'accepting the state, etc., etc.,' the *state* they would have accepted as ultimate arbiter would have been the Kingdom of Sardinia or, say, of Bavaria—and there would have been no Risorgimento at all *or* a movement for German unification.

"To me nineteenth-century European nationalism was 'acceptance of the nation as the only ethical foundation of the state.' And the Risorgimento was the struggle for building an Italian state out of the Italian nation.

"I suggest that you find a new expression to indicate what you call a nationalist. If the Aristotelian flavor does not disturb you, why not call it 'the Western political animal?' I would then be prepared to take Machiavelli as the originator of the ideology."

Mr. Ali Mazrui, for his part, looked inside the concept of nationalism to raise questions concerning the internal coherence and ordering of the elements from which the definition was derived.

"Social transformation in the new states raises questions about the interrelationships between the four categories of nationalism given in *Expectant Peoples*—nationalism as (a) a legal principle; (b) a symbol; (c) an ideology, and (d) a social value. Which of these presupposes which other? Which two are mutually exclusive? Or are they stages in a process of development?

"It has been implied that nationalism as 'social value' is that

nationalism which makes possible a supra-class free market of
ideas. Such a sense of nationalism may be quite incompatible
with nationalism as ideology should the ideology be a simple
monopolistic idea. On the other hand, the ideology may be the
instrument by which political integration is forged. It then
becomes possible to have nationalism as social value following
an integrative ideological nationalism.

"It does not seem to me to be correct to say that legal
nationalism is of interest only to international lawyers. [Silvert
had suggested that the legal aspects of the subject were of the
least moment for the purposes both of book and conference.]
Legal principles like sovereignty are not easily separated from
the symbolism of nationalism like flags and even the symbol
of the frontier or the boundary. And the symbolism may in
turn be inseparable from ideological nationalism."

Mr. David E. Apter objected to the style of the formulation
—the use of a definition to describe a particular unit (the
nation-state), which tempts one to build answers into the definition itself instead of using the definition to suggest criteria in
order to locate specific cases illustrative of aspects of the matter under study. For example, loyalty and disloyalty, affection
and disaffection are matters intimately involved in the definition of nationalism. These are phenomena that suggest empirical propositions and the method by which they may be tested.
After locating these characteristics, one may then enter the
problem of boundaries between the differing varieties of these
happenings; only then do the concrete units or groups get into
the matter.

Naturally Silvert tried to defend his formulation against
these arguments. He found nothing with which to disagree in
the Borsa construction, having assumed that his definition of
nationalism presumed the acceptance only of a certain kind of
state—that which gains its legitimacy precisely from being a

government for *all* inside the national community whether other elements of the culture (such as language) are held in common or not. To fight an antinational state, in this sense, is then a blessing in the eyes of the nationalistic gods; but to fight a truly national state becomes treason. This very problem of readjustment of concepts is being faced by the leaders of almost all the new nations, converted from revolutionaries to antirevolutionaries as they assume the mantle of sovereignty.

The appendix to *Expectant Peoples* contains an attempt to show how the various constituent elements of nationalism may vary in their relationship to each other. Mazrui's point is indeed important if the definition is to be useful at all in dynamic situations—if it is to be more than a mere static description of a given already extant unit, such as Sweden. There must certainly be times when nationalistic ideologies burn at fever pitch but when few persons have a profound commitment to a secular, impersonal nation-state as a working institution. Indeed, this case describes most immediately postcolonial countries. Silvert argued that he was on the one hand setting up an ideal-type description of the "perfect" national polity and against this measure trying to show elements of deviation in the "real-types" by offering up actual cases to reveal differing mixes of the components of the total definition of nationalism. This device has its limitations, of course, for it can measure only the existence of one or another piece of the statement of nationalism as given; it cannot define what a totally non-national society is, nor is it designed to do that job.

Apter's approach remained in contradiction. He suggested other types of criteria. For example, he said, one useful distinction for dividing developing countries may be to examine industrializing vs. modernizing societies. In the first case the independent variable is likely to be economic, while in the latter the problem of fitting and adjusting nonindigenous roles to a new structure assumes a political dimension. Modernization might be considered a particular form of development and "industrialization a special case of modernization." Although a society might hope to do so, it seems clear it cannot achieve industrialization without modernization. The question remains, of course, whether it can modernize without industrializing. Apter proposed other possibilities for building categories of developing countries. For example, he might use coercion and information as governing variables, permitting him to define reconciliation and mobilization systems and such intermediate forms as modernizing autocracies which "traditionalize" innovation.

Many other terms remained at issue, of course. A tendency to make "modernization" and "Westernization" synonymous was quickly combatted by Mr. Yusuf Ibish, who thought any such equation revealed ethnocentrism. Mazrui supported Ibish, structuring his view in this matter:

"Social changes in non-Western states may be of the nature of:

"(a) *Westernization:* This tends to be a total kind of transformation and takes the form of comprehensive emulation. African nationalism passed through this stage of trying to assert equality with the West by suppressing everything African—and trying to be as Western as possible.

"(b) *Modernization:* The emulation in this is no longer comprehensive. On the contrary, there is a distinct attempt to modernize without Westernizing—to do away with, say, chiefs without replacing them with Western representative institutions. The modernization may take the form of experiments in 'basic' or 'guided' democracies or in new forms of one-party rule.

"(c) *Industrialization:* This is often a narrower form of modernization—trying to industrialize without upsetting traditional social institutions too much. Pre-war Japan may have been trying to do just this.

"Anyone who, on the one hand, says there is no difference between 'modernizing' and 'Westernizing' and on the other talks of a 'non-modern Western society' like Spain is contradicting himself. The term 'Western' is too broad if it includes Spain, the USSR, the USA, and pre-industrial Britain. Was England 'Westernizing' herself in the eighteenth and nineteenth centuries?"

Many other subjects were raised. Everyone spoke in these opening sessions, and every subject which was later returned to for more exhaustive discussion was tentatively related to the basic theme—by free association if not by explicitly rationalized reference. Here are some of the major themes:

1. What categories are to be used in ordering the world's polities? In addition to the approaches already given, Mr. Leonard Reissman stated that he would be content with four fundamental measures: industrialization, urbanization, the rise of nationalism, and the rise of the middle sectors.

2. What is to be the relation between the use of the instruments of development and the preservation of cultural integrity? Ibish argued strenuously for a respect for and use of traditional values in the development process. Mr. Khodadad Farmanfarmaian stated that the nexus was impossible and that even were some accommodation feasible, insufficient time and knowledge exist to permit the patience and omniscience required for such a task.

3. What is the role of the elite in development? This question, first posed by Mr. Des Alwi, stemmed logically from Farmanfarmaian's statement and thus immediately turned in upon itself, to burst forth later on many occasions.

4. What are the ethical and political components involved in authority and development? This question was immediately raised by Reissman after Silvert's opening remarks about the possible relationship between pragmatic, "open" patterns of decision making and development. It may as well be confessed here that the problem was never satisfactorily handled, although the discussions on religion acted as a partial substitute for unsnarling other ethical dilemmas.

5. How are comparative approaches to be devised? How is the historical approach to be reconciled with the discussions? A tacit agreement appeared: we did indeed compare and played free with historiography as well as with all other social science methods—including personal reminiscence about the bad bureaucrats we have known. In these first discussions Argentina, Brazil, Lebanon, Italy, Great Britain, Kenya, China, Japan, and many other countries were used as examples and "behavioralists" communicated with "historians." Mr. Yoichi Itagaki exemplified the agreement to compare by not concerning himself with the methodological and conceptual discussion among Silvert, Reissman, Apter, and Mazrui. Instead he put a diagram on the blackboard tracing the historical progression of political and economic development followed by the modern states, against which he promised later to measure the Japanese case.

In sum, the first day cast all the dice in our possession; the participants assumed an identification that they only deepened and extended with time and talk. Mr. Charles F. Gallagher characterized one set of the debaters in such fashion as also to give the tone of the several approaches to the subject. "We have been confronted with a psychiatric process," he said, "wherein Silvert was the theorist suggesting possible lines of diagnosis and Apter was the practitioner who triggered in Ibish, the patient, the problem of identity. Now we can ask ourselves whether we are cured, whether we can all be doctors, or whether we are all still patients."

II. A THEORY OF THE NATION, CONTINUED

In retrospect, the third session—the morning of the second day—was the low point of the entire meeting in terms of morale and simultaneously the beginning of the recuperation. The excitement of the first day, eventuating in so many snips and snaps of themes, ceded on the second to attempts at overarching interpretations which prompted requests for a consideration only of specific cases and for the accumulation of data before essaying the risks of interpretation. Mr. James Eayrs, for example, pleaded against trying to work out a grand theory. He exemplified his argument by referring to an earlier comment that merely teaching Portuguese to an Angolan was not to make him a modern man. Eayrs added that the language, however, certainly opened up for the Angolan a channel of access to the "metropolitan" world. His point was that the meeting would be more fruitful were we to study exactly what happens to the Angolan first—and to Tunisians, Javanese, *et al.*—allowing each member of the conference to draw his own generalizations. Borsa, also dismayed at the seeming disarray of the moment, proposed that each individual make a comprehensive statement on what he considered relevant to the subject and that then the group could wrangle. These suggestions were not formally treated, the unvoiced agreement being to go ahead as before on the assumption that order would emerge from self-imposed discipline. As in the problems of comparison and agreement on terms, the group easily and quickly voted confidence in itself and its ability to discriminate concepts and reconcile differences.

Mr. Juan Gómez Millas chaired this session, and it was the style of his analysis which helped the group to reach a new

plateau of achievement, an accomplishment which gave everyone a glow of satisfaction by the time the afternoon session
ended. Gómez Millas analyzed some of the major schools of
thought dealing with the organization, meaning, and functions
of the nation: *

"A philosophical view of politics requires a comparative historical analysis of institutions and processes in different parts
of the world, in different societies, and during different periods. An equal requirement exists for an historical and philosophical anthropology, which shows the nature of human action both individually and collectively, and in terms of the
historical process. In the same way, a philosophical political
science reaches the frontiers of the metaphysical when it attempts an ultimate determination, a total generalization.

"Biological racism, historical materialism, and other general
explanations are forms of the attempt to arrive at the ultimate
moving forces of the historical political process—from the
most rudimentary polities to the most developed and complicated ones. Today's social scientist does not employ this approach in his work methods, and he does not fall into creating
a system of practical advice. The present tendency of political
science is to build techniques which permit the understanding
of the subjects being analyzed and the transmission of information and intellectual experience.

"The great prestige of natural science, its methods and styles
of work and thought, have led many social scientists to search
for their methodology there and to apply it to sociopolitical
phenomena. Others have sought clues in psychological or psy-
choanalytic tools. None of these methods is really free of seri-

---

* Gómez Millas gave Silvert carte blanche to edit his remarks. "Sum-
marize them, correct them, etc.," were his instructions. For the sake of
clarity only a few paragraphs have been deleted from his original version,
and editing has been restricted mainly to correcting a few words which
have different meanings in English from Spanish.

ous conceptual faults. Another methodological tendency stems from what Dilthey called 'Sciences of the Spirit,' in which the notion of cause and effect is seen in a series of intercrossed lines which give conceptual meaning to political activity (*Spann-Kategorienlehre*).

"Modern political science found in Hegel one of the most powerful and suggestive philosophical influences of the nineteenth century. He revised sociopolitical thought and the systematic approach to it; he reacted strongly against artificial and abstract conceptions of human nature and of the origin and development of political institutions. He is one of the originators of the naturalistic view of the state and an ecumenical understanding of history. He conceived a social ethic in opposition to that of Kant and attacked Liberal ideas of free competition in the market place, affirming the interdependence of the socioeconomic needs of families, groups, and classes. With great fidelity to Greek thought, he conceived of the state as the supreme organizer of cultural life, the guarantor of human security under the rule of a hereditary charismatic chief and sovereign. He glorified the idea of a national state, independent and fortified by the material and spiritual incitement of war. The moment that the state takes for itself all law and morality it has no other power over itself. Among states, only natural law reigns; only divine will can regulate the play of forces and behavior among states. Universal order can be forced on the world only by a state which is able to dominate the others and which represents the universal spirit; having the capacity, that state also has the right to establish itself as legitimate sovereign.

"If Hegel laid the Romantic philosophical cornerstone of the modern nation-state, Rodolf Kjellen added the contribution of all the sciences to the growth of the universal nation-state as international empire. His observations of the events of the end of the nineteenth century and the first quarter of the twentieth century, as well as his study of Ratzel's political geography, convinced him that mere juridical considerations were insufficient to explain the phenomena preoccupying political scientists. He studied the state as power in action in the world political arena. This approach presumed an analysis of spiritual as well as material resources; as a result we have his realistic work on the nations as great powers. Later, in *The State as Life Form* and *Grundriss zu einem System der Politik,* political science is taken to mean the study of the state as an organism whose principal attribute is power. The fundamental originality of Kjellen's organic theory of the state is really his use in a co-ordinated and integrated manner of the conclusions and data accumulated by the many specialized branches of the natural and culturological sciences. His ideas have obviously had great influence on geopolitical thinking in the broader landscape of *Machtpolitik* [power politics].

"In tandem with the great transformation of the modern age dating from the beginning of the eighteenth century was the dawn of the modern Liberal conception of human relations, institutions, and human beings. In Liberal thought similar laws regulate the development of institutions, states, nations, and individuals, and the motivations of all obey similar impulses. The genesis, growth, and decay of nations are regulated by natural laws. One of them, as we know through the experiences of enlightened absolutism, is that oppression leads only to its opposite—revolution—and stimulates national sentiments against the oppressor. The annexation of foreign territories not only does not crush the spirit of the inhabitants but indeed may awaken and transform it. This result seems to occur even if domination is achieved by means of systems apparently of liberation, as was the case of the European nationalities under the impact of the French Revolution.

"European Liberalism presumed that the formation of national unities can be realized only by the prior and spontaneous consent of the people concerned. So Liberalism conceived of the nation as an autonomous entity capable of self-government and embracing, even if only in principle, the institutional idea of nation-state. The new European nations joined their power with that of the states inherited from the traditional dynastic polities; the new political acts were identified with the authority of the people, thus being legitimized not by identity with a sovereign as such, but with the people as sovereign. Progress, tradition, and reason were thus linked and given fresh significance in the new nation-states.

"In the beginning relations among the new nation-states followed Liberal norms: no nation had the right to penetrate the sphere of another one; the aspirations of subjugated nationalities were stimulated by the nations which were already states, a process which reached its culmination with the Wilsonian principles of self-determination. But when Liberals were secure in their new power, the nation-states again began the power play which had characterized the politics of the absolutist, dynastic states. Expansionist reasoning began to dominate the thinking of the national societies; national power thus inverted its motivations and began to serve the politics of the state. There appeared, in full strength, national policy in the sense that the politics of the nation were at the service of the state.

"The principle of respect for other nationalities was abandoned under the stimulus of the growing vitality of each nation-state and the necessity to expand created by the intense problems generated by 'progress' and the application of science to the solution of practical problems. So began the death agony of the Liberal principle of nationalities. And so appeared imperialism, with the justification that imperialism springs from natural and human laws in the shape of a drive toward a world-nation-superstate. Nationalism from this point on becomes based more on the ideas of the Hegelian state than on the Liberal nationality of the nineteenth century. Superstates now subjugate not only their own national subjects but also foreigners. Mass politics fomented by democratic practice merges with the new conception of the nation-state to give power to disciplined groups ready to conquer and manage the power of the nation-state in order to oppress all competitors in the name of unlimited greatness.

"Meanwhile, the dominated colonial peoples profited by the two World Wars to shake off their dependency on the great powers, as we see in many parts of Asia, Australasia, and Africa.

"Liberalism proceeded to its present position impelled by international conflict to seek aid from peripheral countries. International political rivalry led to broad promises of assistance to the developing world, provoking everywhere the acceleration of anticolonialism. At the same time the growth of industrialization in the developing nations created new social instruments: classes, parties, and ideologies effective in the anticolonial struggle to the extent to which the new elites could muster support. So the new nationalistic movements were born with a revolutionary accent and a marked proletarian tendency, as Toynbee called it, or in a rebellion of masses and colored people as Ortega y Gasset and Spengler named the phenomenon. All of them see this process in a pessimistic light as the retreat of Occidental pre-eminence and hegemony, the loss of what was until 1946 the rule of the Occidental World.

"A most realistic analysis of the events of their time were made by Marx and Engels with the instrument of Hegel's dialectic; they introduced into modern thought a scientific approach to the understanding of social development. Their major principle, their 'principle of realism,' is that, in order to be effective, will, knowledge, and activity depend upon the structural characteristics of the system in which they exist. In the preface to the second edition of *Das Kapital,* Marx wrote:

My dialectical method is not only different from Hegel's, but opposed to it. For Hegel the vital process of the human mind is thought, which under the name of "idea" is converted by an independent subject into a demiurge of the real world, that in turn is only the external form, the phenomenology of the idea. I, on the contrary, think that the ideal is the material world reflected by the human mind and translated into thought. The mystifying aspect of the Hegelian dialectic was criticized by me thirty years ago. . . . Nevertheless, the mystification which dialectic undergoes at the hands of Hegel does not prevent his being the first to present his general kind of work in a conscientious and comprehensive manner. . . .

[Gómez Millas then discussed Marx's notions of determinism, the emergence of social phenomena, temporality, and interaction, and the relation of Marxism to biological and historical materialism. Reasons of space preclude an inclusion of the entire discussion, which will pick up where Marxist concepts of the class and the state come together.]

"Man is born into societies in which property relations already exist; those relations define social classes, among which are conflicts stemming from the differing roles played in the process of production. Those conflicts are inevitable and have little or nothing to do with individual conscience, egotism, or altruism. Class divisions give rise to ideologies of all kinds which express class relations and are designed to maintain or weaken the power of the dominant class, whose ideas must prevail in each historical epoch.

"The material forces of production undergo continuous change, sometimes because of changes in natural conditions

and at other times, as in capitalism, because of the development of new techniques of production. At any given moment
in development, changes in the relationship of the factors of
production can breed conflict concerning the relationship of
existing property that hinders production and social development. If those hindrances become profound, modifications in
property systems may be pushed by revolutionary means and
revolutionary ideologies.

"History, according to Marx, can be but an illustration of
class struggle, and the state as the organ of class repression can
never be neutral. The last episode in this universal struggle
must be a clash between capitalism and the proletariat. The
state, directed by a transitory dictatorship of the proletariat,
will die later; the administrative functions the state then per-
forms in its quality of oppressor will become part of the processes of production. Man will escape from a world of necessity
to enter a world of liberty in which he can build his own social
history.

"The Catholic sociopolitical conception of man and society is
strikingly different from the Marxist one, of course. At the end
of the nineteenth century Pope Leo XIII was moved to express
the Catholic position toward the social problems of that day
and toward what should be the position of men in the framework of modern life. The principal doctrinal points of the
Catholic view now are as follows:

"God has established a natural order which scientific and
technological progress makes evident; man shows his greatness
by discovering that natural order and then creating the means
to use natural forces. This natural order is confronted by the
disorder of human life and of social relations. But the conscience of man can discover human order within himself. This
kind of natural or divine order is not the same as that which
reigns in nature, for in human nature laws must be discovered

to regulate relations within and among political communities toward establishment of the universal political community.

"The basis of all organized community is the principle that all humans are by nature endowed with intelligence and free will, from which are born rights and obligations that are universal, inviolable, and inalienable. Among these rights is that of private property, including the use of the tools of production. But this right implies a social responsibility. In addition, such other liberties as association and speech are required to achieve consensus.

"All men have the right of freedom of movement and choice of the political community in which they will live. The fact of 'belonging' to a given political community neither excludes man from the human community nor deprives him of his quality of citizen of the world community. Man may not be held as object possessed but only as subject, basis, and end of social life. Because rights are linked with natural duties, it is insufficient to recognize the right to the necessities of life if man is not provided them in sufficient quantity. Society, therefore, not only must be orderly but also must provide copious fruits.

"The characteristics of the epoch in which we live are three: (1) Today in all national communities all workers feel that they must not be treated arbitrarily by anyone. They are not irrational objects without liberty but are persons in the economy, the polity, and the general culture. (2) Women have entered public and economic life endowed with their own dignity and with rights and duties equal to those of men in domestic and public life. (3) Because all peoples have attained their political independence, or are about to achieve it, no people will dominate others or obey foreign powers. The idea is everywhere that men are equal and that therefore racial discrimination is unjustified.

"Human relationships require a legitimate authority to safeguard law and to contribute in due measure to the common good. Authority is not uncontrolled force but the faculty to order according to reason, having its roots in sharing in God's authority. Authority is a moral force, and therefore governors must first appeal to conscience—to the duty of each to contribute his part voluntarily to the well-being of all. Authority can force compliance only if it is in relation to the will of God and is a part of it. Laws in contradiction with the divine order lack moral force and make authority degenerate into abuse. The essential duty of public power is to guarantee human rights and facilitate the accomplishment of human duties. Experience shows that when public powers do not act appropriately, the economic, social, and cultural instability of man is accentuated, and rights and duties tend to become meaningless words.

"It is therefore indispensable that the state push economic development in harmony with social progress and that, relative to means, there should be provided food, housing, sanitation, education, adequate conditions for religious life, and the use of leisure. Participants in the process of production should be paid with justice, and the worker should have the ability to feel responsibility toward the enterprise in which he works.

"The same moral law which regulates relations among men must also govern relations among political communities. Racism must be eliminated. Differences among human beings and political communities do not justify the predominance of one man or one group over others but rather oblige the more powerful to help the inferior. Further, the function of public authority is not to enclose the members of a nation within given political limits but to strive for the growth of a total human community. No single state can seek its own profit independently of the others.

"In the matter of the relationship between Catholics and non-Catholics, one must distinguish between philosophical questions concerning man, nature, and the universe and practical measures proposed in public areas. Even if such measures have no Catholic inspiration, the Catholic may follow and support them because such public actions which may be contrary to Catholic doctrine are temporal and may change with given historical situations. Thus it may be wise to establish contacts with non-Catholic public groups—the opportuneness of such contacts and their form and extent being a problem of judgment and prudence. All such steps—as well as all social and political ones—must be taken one by one, not by revolution but by well-planned evolution."

Gómez Millas rounded out his remarks by commenting that all the theories of the nation he had outlined had been derived from the experience of the great powers and that now it was high time to have a theory generated not by the dominant powers, but rather coming from the emergent lands themselves. He suggested that this task might well be under way in our discussions. Mazrui picked up this point immediately in order to underscore the sense of mission which impregnates most ideologically motivated political actions.

"The chairman," Mazrui wrote in a memorandum, "was suggestive in the way he related theories of the nation to political philosophy at large. I was particularly interested in his references to the interrelationships between imperialism and nationalism. In my part of the world today nationalism tends to denote a demand for self-rule. What is apt to be overlooked is that nationalism can manifest itself in a desire to rule others. The chairman set the tone of this discussion by referring to political thinkers. Might I refer to Machiavelli's conviction that a country which is fit for republican self-rule is fit to rule others? Something like the same kind of reasoning was to characterize British imperialism in the nineteenth century—that to be civilized enough for representative government at home was to be civilized enough for a civilizing mission abroad. And Joseph Chamberlain was to boast that the British were 'the greatest of the governing races that the world has ever seen.' British nationalism at the time was a nationalism of empire-building. It was later to collide with an empire-demolishing nationalism from Asia and Africa."

Gómez Millas added that the sense of mission was also present in the Spanish conquest of Latin America, but Silvert protested that notions of mission and even of simple profit have no future unless lurking in the background is the power necessary to make them effective. The internal cohesion and strength flowing from national consensus is what made relatively easy the so-called "second wave" of colonial expansion in the latter part of the last century. Mazrui intervened to add a reminder of Lenin's dictum that imperial expansion is a diversion from internal crises and problems. Silvert thought the dictum inapplicable to Britain after 1871 (the convenience date for that second wave of expansionism), but Borsa argued that Lenin's view seemed to hold for fascist Italy's Abyssinian adventure. That reference carried the argument along into the internal troubles of corporate Italy and, by natural extension, into Argentina under Perón from 1946 to 1955. Mr. Laurence I. Radway then suggested that American history provides a third example of the relationship between nationalism and imperialism. The war between the United States and Mexico would be in the same category as the Italian and British cases under discussion.

This chain of reasoning is summarized here in order to demonstrate that even in this early session selective comparative devices were being used; but Gómez Millas' warning at the beginning of his statement that "a philosophical view of politics requires a comparative historical analysis of institutions" affected the discussion immediately. Mr. Alan W. Horton wondered how important it might be to know how people see themselves as national beings. He pointed out that nationalism has been copied in a variety of ways and that the differences, for example, betwen French- and English-influenced African states are striking. He asked whether we should not attempt to construct a typology of emerging nationalisms. One manner of ordering the phenomena could be by the colonial experiences of the new states and the related class structures peculiar to each country. Gómez Millas added that he could see many strategic angles of approach: the motivations of elite groups, governmental policy, the economic strata of the groups from which the nationalist ideas come, and so forth.

The discussion then digressed into the purposes of constructing typologies and variables. Reissman pointed out that the function of any kind of typology is to achieve a certain amount of comparability. For example, the role of elites is comparable from nation to nation. Apter protested that the function of a typology is to *lead* to variables, while Reissman was starting from them. Clearly, we were at a common methodological inpasse: whether research starts with hypotheses to guide the collection of data, or whether we collect data to permit us to make hypotheses. The first procedure is always open to a charge of circularity; the second is always susceptible to the charge of being undisciplined, wasteful, and productive either of the grandest generalizations or the most piddling ones. Needless to say, we no more could settle this disagreement at the meeting than American academia has been able to settle it in its chain of journals. But the difference in approach did punctuate the exchanges throughout the meeting and, as usual, caused many difficulties in conception.

The problem was important at this meeting for, as has been said, *Expectant Peoples* uses a series of hypotheses good only for phenomena falling within the stated problem area, which is given a fundamentally historical definition. Apter, on the other hand, favored constructions which can be applied to all polities everywhere. To illustrate the difference in practice, Apter would seek to divide polities along some such scale as, for instance, high and low coercion systems. Silvert tried to block off polities by such a major characteristic as class and then to build hypotheses for each group within the larger hypothesis which is the category in the first place. These differing techniques will produce very different research questions, of course, but to dispute about which is "better" is not germane. What is pertinent, however, is that the two focuses (which of course were used by all the others in one or another degree during the discussions) served not only to enliven but also to enlighten.

So ended this most difficult of all sessions. Anthropology professors like to tell their students that the first weeks of a community study are always happy ones—a period of rapid learning and consequent joy. Then comes the problem of adjustment to the long haul, like the seventh to ninth years of marriage. The meeting had gone from euphoria to depression to recuperation in three sessions, and it seemed the worst was over.

III. A THEORY OF THE NATION, CONCLUDED

The sense of order and purpose which had begun to permeate the group was ratified in this session. Mr. Reissman, as chairman, announced his view of the manner in which issues had been resolved. First, in the debate concerning theory versus cases, the discussants clearly preferred to continue to move back and forth between the two to the obvious enrichment of both approaches. Common sense had prevailed. Second, he saw that the debate over method and methodological styles was ended, the bases for communication established. Toleration had prevailed. And third, Reissman assumed the group had now fully accepted the idea of comparability among countries and phenomena. The hunger for generalization was not to be ignored. He then turned the debate toward examining nationalism as identified only with a particular kind of development, his purpose being to bring critical attention to the usefulness of the construction behind *Expectant Peoples.* "We do not," he pointed out, "accept the growth of nationalism as unilineal—it is not historically 'necessary' in the Marxist sense of the term. We examine the process, then, to identify the cultural alternatives possible at particular points in that development." By implication, then, the choice *not* to use any nationalistic devices must also have its consequences in the passage into modernism. Reissman continued:

"Nationalism involves a redistribution of power and power relationships, finally in the form of an industrial class system. Such changes must be legitimated, although the content of such social values will vary during the course of national development. (It is obvious that such values will differ from culture to culture, but these variations are not of relevance to the analysis.) Furthermore, every institution must be implicated in that legitimizing process. Religious dogma and religious beliefs, for example, must be interpreted so as to sustain motivations for development and endow them with the highest morality possible. This can be accomplished either by a drastic reinterpretation of traditional religious beliefs and values or by lesser modifications. Similarly, political and economic institutions are oriented to fit the demands of nationalism, and so, too, all other social institutions. A process of such scope cannot be deliberately manipulated, but the total effect is one of institutional consistency—the convergence of all values and behavior toward a more or less unified whole—if national development is to succeed.

"The nationalizing elite, which of all social sectors tends to be most conscious of its goals, must depend upon mass support in the change. First, because they must somehow make their power legitimate; and second, because they must induce the bulk of the population to change its beliefs, motivations, values, and aspirations to mesh with the 'newer' national goals.

"Seen in this particular perspective, 'the nation' is a goal of massive social reorganization which seeks legitimation in traditional values where possible and seeks legitimation in newer values where necessary."

Reissman's statement started a spirited discussion, rich in allusion to all parts of the world. The clarity and relevance of the many cases thrown into the play made this one of the most sparkling of the discussions.

Apter opened the response to Reissman's exposition. Reissman, it should be noted, assumed a certain institutional setup (in this case concentrating on class) and then worked into a series of suppositions concerning the effects of such organization. Later, for example, Reissman argued, "You can't achieve solidarity without a class system. What we are really confronted with is the problem of legitimation of a new set of beliefs and values. If a middle class becomes committed to nationalism, doesn't it have the problem of establishing new bases of legitimacy? The hypotheses proposed by Apter could be held true in every area of social life." Apter's search for those organizing ideas which indeed can assist in organizing all political behavior was made explicit throughout the session.

Now, to return to Apter's response, he first suggested a re-phrasing. "Let's say stratification instead of class, which is only a particular form of stratification," he proposed, "and consider it as a crucial wedge for entering into any concrete society." Parallel to the distribution of power and prestige, he argued, we might examine the growth of civility, as Gabriel Almond has put it (cf. Almond and S. Verba, *The Civic Culture,*

Princeton: Princeton University Press, 1963), and the points of nonintegration in society. We might thus forecast the consequences of caste and class divisions and of specific combinations of the two. He illustrated this point with differences between French Senegal and Guinea, where there is a system of overlapping of differing hierarchies. The creation of a sense of civic culture gives everybody—or, at least, seems to—a role to play in social life. The symbols used do not mean the same thing to persons in different parts of the hierarchy, and each separate hierarchy appears to produce its own kind of nationalism which competes with the nationalism of others. Apter's conclusion was that hierarchies, even if structurally the same, do not produce the same political and civic cultures. The scientific question, then, must be what alternatives are open for each hierarchy.

Mr. E. A. Bayne and Gallagher interposed questions at this point. The former argued that the differences described by Apter could be explained by the varying stages of development which had been attained in each place as well as by differing degrees of association and involvement with France. The volitional element stemming from the several policies espoused by elites also should be noted. Gallagher added that the comparison between Senegal and Guinea could also be extended to Tunisia and Algeria. Why violence in Algeria and a relatively easy transition in Tunisia?

Apter returned to his line of argument by stating that wherever ideology and aspirations combine to make a simple, manageable solution impossible, people begin to perceive the necessity for a moral rebirth, a millennial feeling that usually focuses upon the nation as instrument of fulfillment. The resulting messianism makes for a political mobilization characterized by the primacy of an exhortative component; politics becomes the search for equality.

Reissman asked that some explanation be given of what impels an elite to discard traditionalism as a satisfactory answer to social questions and to assume other, more "modern" ideologies. In reply, Apter once more cited the difference between French and British colonial administrative procedures—that is, a highly centralized system (the French) as opposed to the local structuring of civic culture of the British. In French colonies even the educational hierarchy was restricted and centralized. The local elite was formed in Paris and often participated in French politics, meaning that nationalism was actually born in Paris. Dakar, for example, was an important center for the campaigning of the Radical Socialist and Socialist parties of metropolitan France. The "educated elite" under French cultural influence became a "mobile carrier of civic culture." They created mass participation as well as the party organizations required to control this social mobilization. In English-speaking West Africa, on the other hand, political life began locally, according to Apter.

Gómez Millas stepped in at this point to relate Peru to the discussion of social structure and national movements. Even though Peru is not a "new" nation in the sense in which the term refers to such countries as Senegal and Ghana, class factors may not be operating in such distinct fashions even today. After independence from Spain, commented Gómez Millas, Peru had two societies: a small Spanish-culture local elite, and an alienated and isolated series of Indian villages. Exploitation was the only link binding Indians to Europeans. The rebellion of Tupac Amaru was thus the uprising of one society against another. Nationalism arose long after the separation of Peru from Spain and after the Indian intersocietal revolts. Today Peruvian nationalism seeks to build an integrated state to amalgamate the old in-groups with those who have always been out. In the first instance, then, it is not class which divides Peru but, in reality, the two separate societies which coexist there. In the past such political movements as APRA (Alianza Popular Revolucionaria Americana) which attempted to unite the two groups failed because of the opposition of powerful institutions, and also probably because the APRA elite was out of touch with the Indian villages.

Mazrui also put an emphasis on racial division and went further to claim that the concept of stratification was too wide to be related usefully to national integration. He complained, "Is it necessary to wait until traditional stratification becomes class structure before we can ask whether a society is able to proceed into national integration?" In extension of his remarks he added:

"That classes are one type of stratification is a distinction which has its uses in analyzing the East African scene. Of the last four East African countries—Kenya, Uganda, Tanganyika, and Zanzibar—Kenya has gone furthest in class formation. This is due to the greater degree of economic modernization which the country has experienced—mass unemployment and all! But race retains a correlation with class and income divisions.

"The Zanzibar revolution will significantly change the social stratification of that society—but probably not in the direction of greater classlessness. On the contrary, Zanzibar will probably now become more of a class society than it was before—though there will be less coincidence between race and income levels than there was before."

The discussion here took a turn into the question of legitimation. That is, with the many social situations to be seen in the world, implying varying ideas and world views held by individuals in many different human situations, how can political action be explained, justified, and rationalized in order to gain consensus? Ibish argued a gulf between elite and the led—that they were speaking two different languages, and that the elite was unleashing a giant, because, intent on development, the elite was disregarding the consequences of the total destruction of the beneficial heritage of traditional and religious life.

Apter then entered the discussion to equate political and church religion and proposed a hypothesis: that modern forms of political religion elevate certain secular ends to a sacred level but do not really achieve the transfer. Political religion and church religion can live together so long as each sticks to its area of concern. But when the secular is opposed to the secular or the sacred to the sacred, we have possibilities of wide conflict and of total social transformation. Gallagher responded that the hypothesis did not work, for the clash arises as soon as the secular becomes more dynamic in a traditional religiously oriented society such as Islam. Ibish returned to state that any ultimate concern—whether having to do with politics or with God—can become an individual's functional religion. Thus began a discussion which was to become the principal preoccupation of several sessions.

Meanwhile, other members of the group, such as Horton, brought the matter back to consensus and legitimation. Silvert re-entered the discussion, too, to outline the case for the relationship between social class as such (not mere stratification of any kind) and national integration. He argued that national community, in the strict functional sense, could never be formed in a situation of caste division and that, indeed, one of the basic "purposes" of nationalism was to bridge and channel the differences which exist in modern class societies. He used Mexico as a case in point, proposing that in that country three general types of social order coexist. One, the modern, covers the usual class spread we see in any industrial society. A second, the traditional, parallels the modern in terms of hierarchy but includes many more rural workers and alienated urban groups at the bottom of the heap. Off to one side are the Indians, segregated by their culture into a castelike relation to the rest of society. This division, however, will not reveal itself if we use standard income-occupation measures of class. And even if we employ the richer Weberian construction of dividing persons into classes by measures of economic, social, and political power, we may have some difficulty in explaining why members of the same class group can be so politically opposed. Why does the Argentine Navy shoot at the Argentine Army?

Silvert's argument was that, for fineness of analysis, classes in transitional countries must also be divided by measures of value systems, or *Weltanschauungen,* to use the once-popular term. Upper-class persons who accept a secular state as the impersonal and ultimate arbiter of secular dispute think and act in politically different ways from those traditionalists who insist on universalistic moral judgments. If anyone wants to apply those now badly misused terms, we might say that we have the Protestant and the Catholic ethics at war within the same class groups and among classes as well.

Silvert argued that these divisions split families, armies, slums, and universities. For example, if we propose to assist persons to better their social positions through aid programs on the presumption that we will thus increase the number of modern folk, so to speak, then we had better find out whether we are merely helping persons to higher power on the traditional ladder. By the terms of this argument, then, Silvert contended that lateral mobility (from Indian to Spanish traditional or modern, and from Spanish traditional to modern) was in its way at least as important as upward mobility.

It is obvious that there must be mechanisms for adjusting clashes in such a complex situation, he argued further. Otherwise the societies would break up. These very shock absorbers,

however, often hinder and sometimes make further development impossible.

And so, without too long a search, we had found our common ground. As Reissman had pointed out, we no longer
scourged ourselves with whether to or how to compare. Also,
we had begun to theorize less and to generalize more, since we
now had revealed several competing theories which could be
referred to in short form ("Apterian," "Ibishian," "Silvertian,"
for example). In brief, a consensual base had been established.
But the conference did not dedicate itself to a mere spelling
out of areas of agreement and disagreement. Instead, we
moved along not only into an extensive comparative review of
cases (and almost *all* the discussion hereafter was comparative) but also into such problems as religiosity versus secularism in social affairs, *Geist* versus pragmatic humanism,
historical mills versus human control, and determinism versus
rationality.

CHAPTER TWO

Searching for Justification and Reason

D. *National Integration and Individual Psychology: Problems of Self-Identity.* The psychology of the nation, especially as it affects elite groups and the transitional social elements. What are the values and attitudes of intellectuals and others which may affect the nation and which can most easily be satisfied only by certain kinds of public activity? Problems of personal aspiration, participation, and satisfaction within the grandly political sphere. What is the impact on national psychological set of such social enclaves as the military, industrialists, and others with at least the techniques of modern organization and sometimes the values thereof? *Chairman: Y. Ibish.*

E. *Economic Development and the Nation.* Autarchy, economic independence, and national identification. Industrialization and urbanization and their relationship to national patterns of social participation. Class structure as affected by occupational structural change, and the impact on the political nation. The order of events—an economic "base" first? *Chairman: E. A. Bayne.*

F. *Economic Development, National Identification, and Leadership.* Leaders of anti-colonialism and leaders of national development. Demagoguery, ideology, social mobilization, legitimacy

49

and consensus, and the growth of the nation. The institutional organization of the state, leadership and interest groups related. *Chairman: K. Farmanfarmaian.*

G. *The Transmission of National Values and Ideologies.* Patterns of acculturation, cultural penetration, the transmission of ideas, practices, and techniques in general, taking into account the history of colonialism and European expansionism from imperialism to missionaries to the United Nations and commercial companies and television. Does the *agency* of cultural transmission have anything to do with content? Has the *period* a decisive influence on content? How determinant is the receiving culture? What has been the actual experience in the transmission of political forms and ideologies and other related matters on nationalism in developing lands? *Chairman: Y. Itagaki.*

H. *Strategies of Nation-Building; Internal Leadership and Social Participation.* A continuation of the preceding two themes, with special attention to the radius of action of nationalizing elites in nation-building, consensus, and the relationship of domestic to international politics. How do the factors of new technology and velocity of change affect the power of elite groups and of other aspiring groups? Again, can typologies of social occurrence be built to permit prediction? *Chairman: Des Alwi.*

I. PROBLEMS OF SELF-IDENTITY AND ECONOMIC GROWTH

A sense of anticipation infused the conference as we prepared to talk about national integration and individual psychology and then about problems of economic development. Although these two subjects may seem to be relatively far apart, another happy accident contrived to make two strong protagonists of almost opposite persuasion the chairmen of two of the three sessions involved. Ibish led the discussion of individual psychology. From the first day he had been cogently arguing that leaders pressing for development should also respect religious and traditional values. Using the example of the extended family as a beneficial traditional device threatened by modernism, he repeated his concern that development may generate social violence if it destroys useful institutions without offering acceptable substitutes.

Opposed to Ibish's respect for traditionalism was Farmanfarmaian's insistence on the absolute necessity of economic development, no matter the costs in shattered images and usages of past social organization. Farmanfarmaian, an intense and articulate practicing economist, reminded Silvert and Gómez Millas of a Mexican in his combination of volatility and seriousness of purpose. No better protagonists of the two points of view could have been found—not least because they had gone to school together, so that a vibrant bond of friendship held them together despite other differences. With great sensitivity the two managed to avoid abstruse arguments based on their association that would have left the rest grasping for understanding. The large number of persons at the meeting professionally and personally involved with Islam (Ibish, Farmanfarmaian, Mazrui, Horton, Gallagher, Des Alwi) sometimes caused the rest of us plaintively to ask for a visa to get into the Muslim discussions, but Islamic collegial cohesion did not prevent others from taking sides in their intramural arguments.

Indeed, a tantalizing four-way split developed because of the Ibish-Farmanfarmaian debates. As traditionalism debated modernism, there also arose the issue of how much human control is possible in massive social events. At first blush it might appear that the economic developers and the professional social scientists would range themselves solidly on the side of the possibilities of human engineering, of managed social change. Not at all! Ibish argued that the ways of traditional society must be well understood before adequately reasonable and rational developmental procedures can be followed. If the past is destroyed with promises of the future, then a sleeping giant will be awakened whose unreasoning thrashing about will destroy the very advances being pursued.

Farmanfarmaian vigorously offered the view that the urge to industrialize is irresistible and that all that can be done is simply to make the economic changes as best we know how, letting the other matters arrange themselves as they will.

Borsa, a historian, allied himself with the Farmanfarmaian school. "History may be man-made," he said, "but not as absolutely man-planned as Ibish seems to be implying." Economic development in such countries as India, he argued, is "a matter of life and death." Development will occur under compulsion, and the necessity to develop is made even more acute by the present population explosion. "There is not much point in thinking what will come after economic development."

Reissman, a sociologist, joined Borsa in these views, but perhaps for different reasons. The social sciences are simply not sufficiently refined for us to be able to engage in careful and broad planning, and so we might just as well go ahead with what we can at least do a little bit—economic development planning—and let the other areas of human experience make their adjustments.

Silvert took his side with Ibish on the issue of the possibilities for a wide range of effective and rational choice. Silvert's argument was that the political kingdom is becoming ever more evidently the seedbed of other social change. Politics implies the making of effective decisions—that is, the application of power to conflict areas. He could see no reason why at least the attempt cannot be made to use the power flowing from certain appropriate aspects of traditional ways in order to push along modernization. In any event, it is probably unrealistic to argue in black and white terms, for in all transitional situations no means exist absolutely to nullify the effects of the traditional order. Is man then so ignorant that he cannot possibly avail himself of as broad a range of social practice as may be consistent with or amenable to modernization? This argument will reappear in changed form at the end of our sessions, so let us turn now to some of Ibish's specific comments.

"The social factor has been the least studied by those concerned with the Middle East," he said in his opening remarks as chairman. "Many of the weaknesses of the states in the region are the result of their failure to diagnose and to meet adequately the prolonged social crisis.

"Middle Eastern society, as a social organism, is the resultant of a great variety of continually changing spiritual and material forces producing strains which require adjustment.

"The state existed before the church in Islam. For two centuries there was no other institution to dispute the monopoly of power enjoyed by the institution of government. The individual stood unprotected and unshielded and helpless before the military might of the state. This was a source of great tension and anxiety.

"The organ evolved by society to adjust the rising tensions resulting from the state's monopoly of power was the religious brotherhood. Through these brotherhoods the church (understood as the community of believers) was organized. Gradually the church amassed enough power to balance the military might of the state, and an inner equilibrium was established. Ultimately the brotherhood encompassed all social classes and reinforced the functional groupings by trade guild and corporation.

"In the nineteenth century this precarious balance was entirely destroyed. It was perhaps destroyed less by the direct intrusion of the West than by immensely complicated internal developments which are not sufficiently studied. Only these things are reasonably certain:

"(i) The old corporative functional groups decayed and dissolved.

"(ii) The old brotherhood organization also decayed.

"These two results led to the loss of the personal link between the individual and the community and of the social and religious integrations.

"(iii) The power of the state was enlarged by:

"a. The increased efficiency of its own instruments, and

"b. The decay of its counterbalancing.

"The cycle is complete and the individual is again standing before the might of the state unprotected and unshielded. This is the essence of the modern Middle Eastern crisis.

"Whether the dissolution of the old community structure will ultimately prove beneficial depends on the principles and forms of social cohesion that will take its place. Rural co-operatives and industrial trade unions are still in their infancy and fail to satisfy the deeper emotional and spiritual needs. The ordinary individual belongs to his family (extended type) and to Islam, but Islam no longer has any concrete social organization. This social void is intensely real and craves a form (Islamic) of expression. The region's volcanic instability is perhaps a symptom of the attempt to find new organs and institutions through which the individual can participate."

Looking at what Farmanfarmaian said, we find no less broad a sweep, but how different a one! He opened his chairmanship by announcing that he was going to descend from the high intellectual plane of previous discussions by stating some propositions that he felt were easily demonstrable. The first was that a world half rich and half poor implies a situation of disequilibrium which cannot possibly last. People who barely subsist no longer accept their fate as inevitable—a fact which the rest of the world does not find as frightening as it should, especially since during the past fifty years the situation of the world's poor has been deteriorating. The second proposition was that the secret of getting rich is out and that it is only a matter of time for this new knowledge to be applied. The reason is plain: all men can learn to use modern technology. Although the application of new techniques for the raising of living standards may be done through disastrous means, it will be done and in a shorter time than most Western social scientists think possible. There are already such models of rapid development as Japan, China, and Soviet Russia to which desperate leaders in the underdeveloped countries can look for example and proof that indeed there are short cuts.

Farmanfarmaian then proceeded to discuss the nature of economic development. The process is nonreversible, he said, and the industrialization which is an inseparable component of generalized economic development carries with it an array of indispensable habits, attitudes, and behavior patterns. He specified his views as follows:

a. There is as yet no prescription for economic development which does not include industrialization.

b. Industrialization demands organization, habits, and attitudes that imply a clear and fundamental break with the past. No compromise with the essence of traditionalism is possible.

c. Utility comes before beauty as a criterion of what is wanted in the culture; hard work replaces leisure.

d. Consumption patterns must change from conspicuous consumption to saving and careful budgeting of resources.

e. Specialization intrudes to break the concept of "universal men" and "universal geniuses," forcing a new definition of individualism which must be compatible with the co-operation required among specialized persons.

The primal urge toward development seen by Farmanfarmaian has its effects not only in economic, aesthetic, and political matters but also involves the basic commitment to become the equals of developed men everywhere. "The world is reform and restoration," he fervently said in defense of his position.

"Leadership over the next ten to twenty years must respond to urges for development from whatever sources they come and must conspicuously serve as a vehicle for speedy development if it is to survive."

Ibish and Farmanfarmaian provided the parentheses for these long discussions. In between there was ardent debate and the formalized presentation of case examples by other persons. But also there was the chairmanship of Bayne, who offered a conditioned viewpoint about the role of economics in the total development process which did not make its full impact on the discussants at the time. As we have seen, Ibish talked of what should be done, Farmanfarmaian of what will be done. Ibish proposed caution, reason, and care. Farmanfarmaian proposed dash, intelligent "feel," and action. Ibish respected old philosophical values and new conveniences, Farmanfarmaian old aesthetic achievements and a new way of life. Ibish wanted a frontal attack on total social problems; Farmanfarmaian thought possible only an intensive attack on industrialization. Bayne, for his part, moved into no inane "middle" position. He proposed to explore precisely the nature of the relationship between economic and other kinds of development.

His argument was that economic development is a necessary but insufficient condition for complete modernization. Economic development can provide part of the framework for modern nationhood, but economic integration and rationalization do not imply the automatic flowering of political integration and rationality. Economic development thus has no magical effect in producing a modern society, even if it does provide a modern physical-economic setting. Italy's "economic miracle," for example, has not been accompanied by equal political and social maturation. The paternalistic pattern of class relationships has changed but little and still remains tied to such a seeming anachronism as strong regional differences in interclass behavior, despite the existence of factories in many parts of the land. The basic array of choices exercised by the Italian industrial worker is still very narrow.

Bayne then changed his focus from Italy to Israel, where the addition of large numbers of Sephardic immigrants has created problems of caste and class integration despite the pre-existing strength of national integration in the Jewish state during its early years. Further economic development is being sought in Israel, not for its own sake alone, but also as a device to permit the transformation of the newly arrived unskilled migrants into participant and productive members of the economy. In the meantime, efforts at cultural integration continue. Israel is seeking a forward move toward a superior level of integration, even if in encouraging non-European migration it temporarily took a step backward. The point is that the Israelis recognize the problem to be much more than merely economic and are seeking to change persons in many different ways and through many varied avenues.

Some of the discussion surrounding these three essays was formally stuctured. The Arabist Legion, for example, extruded a phalanx to present a prepared series of cases organized to be comparative not only for the intrinsic descriptive merit of the examples but also explicitly to test parts of the *Expectant Peoples* construction.

Gallagher opened his discussion of the Tunisian situation by carefully describing how a constant compression of the social classes has been taking place there since independence. The removal of French control ripped away an upper group, in part nonresident, of course. But the national government of Tunisia since then has not attempted a rearrangement of class order, instead reducing the psychological as well as economic distance dividing the social layers. Gallagher then described the new participation-creating institutions and organizations which are, in effect, also "creating new individuals." He defined "participants" as persons who pay attention to public matters or, especially in today's Tunisia, to the interminable laws, prescriptions, and decrees issued by the government. Party members, trade unionists, educated persons, and those involved in civil and military service and public works projects and, very importantly, the liberated women comprise the newly integrated national Tunisians. Probably three-quarters of the total population of four million are now participant. Gallagher then described the institutional means being used to create this sense of belonging, giving great emphasis to the school system and to the seemingly tireless activity of political men in mobilizing the population into all manner of actvities—"busybodyness," as he put it.

Tunisia's official Neo-Destour Party has long been active in rural areas, operating in a way that no other Arab party has as yet been able to accomplish, according to Gallagher. The resulting social amalgamation may not be so complete as in Cuba, but certainly the costs have not been so high. Then, to the intense satisfaction of Silvert, Gallagher turned to the appendix of *Expectant Peoples* and applied the model described there of the changing relations among nationalism as symbol, ideology, and value as national polities mature. He reached the conclusion that Tunisia politically seems now to have entered upon the beginning of true national integration: a secular state which can command consensus, legitimacy, and legal power. The ideologies of the nation are losing their shrillness, and the symbols being manipulated refer to work and nation-building and a new kind of individualism. Tunisia is now also becoming primarily concerned wth domestic development, "being one of the Arab countries with the strongest national component, and this without stressing its international allegiance to the Arab world." Individual push and creativity have, in a certain sense, suffered. Nevertheless, Gallagher is of the opinion that Tunisia is the only country of Arab North Africa which has unmistakably crossed the line into modern national organization. He then posed his key and concluding question. Given grave economic difficulties and a population explosion, it would appear that raising per capita income will be very difficult. Can this society continue to develop along ever increasingly modern lines and yet remain poor? Or will the political modernization in itself make it possible to break the economic bind?

This question was permitted to wait for its answer until Horton had discussed the case of Egypt since 1952. He too based his discussion upon the class and value model proposed by Silvert. Of those in the upper group of Egyptian society before the Nasserist revolution, perhaps only one-eighth were of modern mentality, the remainder firmly traditional in view. Aided by a traditional bureaucracy, they controlled a politically listless country, although certainly the urban areas sometimes showed signs of social and economic yeastiness. Only in religious matters had this group changed, becoming secularist as a partial substitute for a completely modern attitude of political relativism and tolerance.

Under this aristocracy were ethnic minorities which in their size and importance were peculiar to Egypt. These minorities formed isolated and exclusivistic communities of their own, contemptuous of all that was Arab and clinging tenaciously to their languages and traditions. The urban poor, if they had any organization at all, divided themselves along traditional communal lines, as did the landless rural people. The relationship among these strata was entirely paternalistic, with no shadow of an impersonal national feeling to sully this landscape of traditional light and shadow.

Nasser's revolution was a complete destruction of the old elite and a thorough shaking up of the ethnic mosaic, most of whose members have left Egypt. The few remaining are now subjected to forced linguistic integration, especially through the educational system. The spearhead of the drive for modernization remains the military, although it is hampered by a bureaucracy which is still largely traditional. A new class element is being added as the government has attempted recently to attract Western-trained intellectuals and engineers, types now being presented as "culture heroes."

After these two analyses the discussion moved to a comparison of Tunisia and Egypt and then back to the question concerning poverty and political modernization posed by Gallagher. Silvert optimistically volunteered the idea that human beings are the basic economic as well as political and social resource. Therefore, to establish conditions which liberate men's talents is also to create the pre-condition for increased productivity—always assuming that at least some natural resources can be found to work on. Capital accumulation, in this view, is a dependent variable of the other two factors, and particularly of the attitude of a population toward productivity and saving. This venture seemed to jibe with Gallagher's view, and the session adjourned, ready for the direct confrontation with economic matters already described.

II. THE TRANSMISSION OF CULTURAL VALUES

Japan is the world's one "non-Western" country now almost universally deemed to be a developed nation. The reasons for Japan's modernization are, of course, of fascination to social scientists everywhere. In addition, Japan's role in Asia as a "non-Western Westernizing" influence also presents fertile fields for research—and in this case the fields are virtually unworked. Therefore Mr. Itagaki was asked to address himself to the latter question, the presumption being that he could also be exploited during the discussions to help us with the first. This supposition turned out to be correct. Itagaki prepared a careful presentation on the transmission of cultural values, and then the discussion turned both on patterns of colonialism and the special case of Japanese development.

Mr. Itagaki, who in the past had himself been a colonial administrator, took a cool view of his subject but underneath revealed as great a concern with fundamental value and world-view systems as Ibish. Because Itagaki thought his English weak, he was diffident during the first days of discussion. He therefore prepared a detailed written statement, which an impromptu team of participants mimeographed for him so that it might be distributed in advance of his exercising the chair. It should be added, however, that Itagaki's English later proved entirely sufficient for active debate and that he had no difficulties as chairman.

Itagaki divided his paper into two parts, the first the establishment of a theoretical frame of reference, and the second an analysis of "Westernization and Patterns of Nationalism in Non-Western Countries." Because reproduction of both parts here would be ungainly, the second section will be quoted in its entirety, and the theoretical portion will be summarized in order to provide at least some taste of Mr. Itagaki's style of thought.

He began by asking "what is really meant by civilization." Leading the group through Spengler, Toynbee, Frankfort, Benedict, Kroeber, and Sorokin, he pointed out that all of them introduced one or another concept of style in attempting to delineate the heart or core of what is special to a civilization. Although particularly complimentary of Spengler, Itagaki argued that "the greatest drawback of his theory is that it left no room for the consideration of transmissions and interactions between civilizations."

He therefore turned to an examination of Alfred Weber and his "more systematic study of the inner structure of civilization." Itagaki pointed out that Weber presumed that only those values can be transmitted which have a certain universality. Thus, cultural values cannot truly be carried from one society to another in their basic forms. Such "world religions" as Christianity and Buddhism "have a certain possibility of being transmitted beyond their places of origin . . . only when and if their essential religious truth has such inner 'universality' as the salvation of the human soul." The transmission of this special kind of cultural value must be distinguished from the universality of science and technology, which is based on their "logical and universal validity." It is obvious that ideas at the empirical level can be most easily carried from one civilization to another.

Toynbee was the next major scholar considered by Itagaki, who said of him, "Among many scholars of civilization, Arnold Toynbee has made a remarkable contribution by introducing his thoroughgoing observations in the area of the dynamics of civilization and acculturation, instead of becoming entangled with the problems of 'style of civilization' or 'culture-patterns.'" Itagaki found particular utility in Toynbee's elucidation of the manner in which "all the different elements in a culture-pattern have an inner connection with each other and form an indivisible or an organic whole." Therefore, when the process of contact between civilizations starts, there also begins to work a "law governing the process of cultural radiation and reception." Itagaki explained that this notion "means that when a culture-ray of a radioactive civilization gets diffracted into its component strands (economic, political, linguistic, intellectual, technological, scientific, philosophical, artistic, religious, and so forth) by the resistance of a foreign social body, those strands that are the most trivial in cultural value receive the least resistance from the society impinged upon and tend to penetrate faster and farther than the others. This explains the commonly observed fact that technology, for instance, achieves a faster and wider penetration than religion."

Itagaki then proceeded to explain how what may seem superficial actually seeps into a society and works primary changes. This effect occurs because of the essentially organic nature of the body social, which must react as a whole to even light stimuli. Further, what may be a benign factor in the originating civilization can have disastrous effects in the receiving one.

Toynbee's theories of possible reaction to foreign acculturative influences were then also described by Itagaki. He mentioned the "Zealotist" reaction of fanatic rejection, as opposed to the "Herodian" utilization of the weapons of the intruding civilization for protection against the original inventors and owners of the weapons. "However, we have to remember that, even if the Herodians could escape from the destiny of defeat—which is the Zealots' lot—they are also doomed to conversion in the end to the way of life of the alien civilization, through the process of Toynbee's laws of 'cultural radiation and reception.'"

Itagaki continued, "Aside from the self-defeat of both Zealotism and Herodianism, there also lies open a middle way of salvation in which a mutual adjustment between the old order and the new departure can arrive at a harmony on a higher level . . . Toynbee writes about this possibility of choice which is, so to speak, a 'synthesis of culture,' as 'Evangelism,' but it will become feasible only by the emergence of some new dynamic force or creative movement from within the society concerned."

The last element in this theoretical discussion concerned the forms of cultural transmission. Here Itagaki turned to Danilowski for his inspiration, explaining the three forms of cultural transmission seen by him. First is "transplantation," the simple movement of civilization from one area to another, as in the case of the English migration into Australia. The second is "implantation," which Itagaki called "comparable to the grafting of an apple tree onto a pear tree. In this case the grafted alien civilization dwells parasitically in the indigenous civilization . . . the grafted tree (alien civilization) never changes the character of its substance in the least. At any rate the apple tree is an apple tree and the pear tree is a pear tree . . . The native tree only transfers nutrition to the implanted one and gets no advantage . . . Therefore, this can be called the most miserable and unproductive type of transmission of civilization."

Danilowski's third form Itagaki called "soil improvement." It is the most productive one in that an alien civilization has a favorable effect on the indigenous civilization. "The native civilization takes nutrition from the alien civilization and improves the native soil . . . In this case the various results of alien civilization serve for the development of the indigenous one as material and means."

In closing this part of his presentation, Itagaki returned to his agreement with most of the authorities he had cited that the fundamental core, the bases of a civilization, cannot be transmitted to others. In order to maximize the communication of those elements which can truly pass between cultures, then, "the transmission should be done creatively, based on the receiver's own fundamental understandings. By doing so the borrower will be able to obtain a fruitful effect through contact with alien civilizations." This construction was used by Itagaki as the key to his discriminating between the effects of European influences on Japan and on other portions of Asia and particularly Southeast Asia.

Let us now pick up Mr. Itagaki's text as he moved toward the application of these hypotheses to selected countries of Asia.

"1. *Westernization in terms of colonization.*

"It was our intention to try to set up a frame of reference to approach our subject, and this is why we have examined in some detail representative theories of culture contact and acculturation. Now we shall proceed to the problems of culture contact and political acculturation in the non-Western world, especially in the South and Southeast Asian countries, in terms of the frame of reference we have just built.

"The first and foremost thing is that any of the problems of encounters between civilizations after the fifteenth century in these areas can be considered as a problem between the modern West and the non-West. And any impulse of challenge was given from the Western side, to which response was made from the non-Western side.

"The second important thing is that the processes of challenge and response were historical facts backed by conquests and colonizations, not by free and peaceful relations, in spite of being recognized as Westernization of the non-West in terms of transmission of civilization. Even in the countries which had kept themselves from the fate of being colonized, it seems to me that their windows were opened toward Westernization only for their own survival under the persistent threat, pressure, and fear of colonization. Under the circumstances Westernization was inevitable for them. While Zealot countries were defeated and hence colonized, Herodian countries could manage to continue to exist and remain independent and autonomous. The term 'Westernization' actually means, in any case, Westernization associated with colonization.

"Thirdly, in connection with the second part, it is of importance for the forms of cultural transmission and reception to know whether the society accepting Western cultural values is autonomous or under colonial rule. The former has a somewhat greater spontaneity and free choice in cultural acceptance, while the latter has no opportunities of choice under colonial force and coercion. Accordingly, cultural transmission in the colonial societies had no alternative but to take the form of '*Aufpropfung*' (implantation) in the terminology of Danilowski. In this case Westernization did not discharge any productive function. On the contrary, it may be considered that the autonomous societies, such as Russia in the eighteenth century, Japan in the nineteenth, Turkey in the early twentieth, and so on, had greater opportunities to realize Westernization in the context of '*Bodenverbesserung*' (improvement of the soil).

"2. *Cultural dualism and transmission of national political values.*

"Proceeding from the fundamental reflections based on the premises stated above, we shall observe, in the main, what has come into existence as a result of cultural transmission in the form of 'implantation' mainly in the colonial societies. It may be summarized as follows: what Westernization as colonization has produced is cultural, social, political, and economic dualism or pluralism.

"In the next place, what are the characteristics of the political aspects of acculturation? And what kind of national political values were introduced into dependent societies? To my way of thinking the most basic national political values implied in the idea of the modern nation-state of the West seem to be the threefold concept of national independence, political unity, and democratic freedom. These value concepts had been established in the historical process of endogenous development of Western societies during about three hundred and fifty years from the Renaissance and Reformation in the fifteenth and sixteenth centuries to the French Revolution and Industrial Revolution in the late eighteenth century and the early nineteenth century. When the Western colonial empires engaged in colonizing activities in a most systematic way, these three basic concepts had been already self-evident for them. But the concepts of national independence and political unity were excluded from transmission, because it was the first principle of colonization not to give these two concepts to colonies. However, there was inevitably a transmission of the concept of democratic freedom to the colonial societies as a concomitant of having introduced economic liberalism in these areas in order to pursue the economic interests which were the original purpose of colonization. But it should be noted that the concept of democratic freedom transmitted into colonial societies had nothing to do with the problem of the legitimacy of political power or the authority of colonial rulers. In this sense the transmission of the concept was rigidly in the form of 'implantation.' Accordingly, any form of democratic political institutions established in the colonial societies for the implementation of democratic freedom was distorted. Nevertheless, it can safely be said that the concept of democratic freedom was the only one which was transmitted in the course of Westernization during the colonial period.

"3. *The Developmental Patterns of Asian Nationalism.*

"(a) *Colonial Period:* Asian nationalism arose generally from the late nineteenth to the early twentieth century and, as a whole, followed a two-phase development in the colonial period. The early phase of development of colonial nationalism

bears the following aspects: the first is that of cultural nationalism, and the second is that of a movement that demanded
from their colonial rulers the removal of obstacles to sound
development of the concept. Their demand was, in a word,
nothing but a desire for social equality or a desire for social
nondiscrimination in terms of democratic freedom.

"The later phase of colonial nationalism was promoted by
political leaders who had realized that the wholesome development of democratic freedom could not be fully achieved without attaining national independence and political unity. For
this reason they were fervently aware of no alternative to re-
moving the colonial rulers in order to achieve the sovereign
independence of their own nation. Political nationalism allied
with a desire for political independence developed in this
phase, and irreversible anticolonialism proceeded.

"Needless to say, the promoters of these movements were
indigenous intelligentsia. They were those who had fully
learned the intrinsic national political values of Western nationalism. In this way almost all colonial countries in Asia
achieved independence after World War II.

"(b) *Post-Independence Period:* the problem of periodization of this stage seems to be difficult for us because the independence of new states in Asia was achieved successfully from
1946 (the Philippines) to 1957 (Malaya), and they are still in
fluid transition. If I may venture to generalize, it should be
noted that the year 1958 is supposed to be a remarkable water-
shed in the political scenes of most Asian countries. The pre-
1958 phase was the period during which political democracy
had been tested, and the post-1958 phase is the period during
which a remarkable tendency can be seen toward authoritarianism, symbolized by the emergence of a modernizing military
oligarchy substituted for a decaying constitutional democracy.
Let us now consider the alteration of political systems from the

one to the other in the context of transmission of national political values.

"The problem which post-independence nationalism in Asia confronted was the achievement of national political unity and democratic freedom. At this moment, it should be recalled clearly that political institutions of the Western democratic pattern had been already implanted to a greater or lesser degree before independence and had operated in a limited and distorted form within an iron frame of political unity imposed by the colonial power. In addition, it has also to be recalled that the preservation and maintenance of constitutional or parliamentary democracy had been, so to speak, imposed by suzerain powers upon the new states as one of the essential conditions of the transfer of sovereign power. As a matter of fact, almost all independent countries in Asia made efforts in the direction of democratic ideas and institutions based on Western patterns of constitutionalism. But it became clear between 1956 and 1958 that Western political institutions were neither workable nor effective in these new states. A major cause is the lack or weakness of national political unity, which is a precondition of democratic freedom.

"For the establishment of national political unity, there must exist an authority of some kind, and this authority must be a symbol of national cohesion or national political consensus. Here arises one of the basic political problems, namely that of legitimacy of political authority. The Western pattern for the solution of this problem of legitimacy has been to establish representative institutions on a basis of political competitiveness, political participation, civilian rule, and so on, which are closely associated with democratic political values. But historically it took no less than three hundred years to achieve. However, a two-stage development was required. The first stage was that of 'centralized unity' called 'absolutism' in the political sphere and 'mercantilism' in the economic sphere. The next stage of democratic freedom was called democracy politically and liberalism economically.

"Not only has the independence of Asian countries not automatically brought about political unity, but it is also nearly impossible to create political unity from the prejudiced ideas and distorted institutions of democratic freedom inherited from the pre-independence period, for they were only the products of 'implantation.' The primary and pressing task for the new states is the creation and strengthening of political unity. But for the sake of its ultimate realization, it is rather necessary to attach less value to democratic freedom, regarding it as second in importance to political unity. This is clearly illustrated by the decline of constitutional democracy in 1958. As a consequence, the strengthening of charismatic authority has emerged as a substitute. Attention is, at present, focused on national political centralization rather than legal legitimacy.

"*4. The Revolutionary and 'Eclectic' Character of Asian Nationalism.*

"Lastly, I would like to refer briefly to two distinguishing characteristics of Asian nationalism in the post-independence period.

"The first one is its *revolutionary character*, determined chiefly by the following three causes. Firstly, there is a psychological climate of impatience among people, who can no longer rely upon the orderly process of gradualism. Because no noticeable improvement of living conditions has taken place after independence, an urgent need for economic development is emphasized. Secondly, chasms and rigidities of social-economic dualism (which are in large part colonial vestiges) seem the major impediments to the rapid realization of national economic values in terms of national economic integration. That is why revolutionary measures, as illustrated by hastily executed nationalization policies, are occasionally adopted. Thirdly, there is little relief from discontent and frustration about present conditions as long as they follow the same principles of capitalism and liberal democracy as the Western nations. In this case, as an effective counterattack to Westernization, they search for alternative means and may adopt socialism, communism, and totalitarianism based upon principles contrary to those of Westernization. This can be thought a kind of 'futurism,' a concept from Toynbee (VI, p. 97) which means taking a flying leap out of the present into an uncertain future.

"The second distinguishing characteristic of Asian nationalism is, to use Francis Carnell's terminology, that of 'eclecticism.' This eclectic character has not yet become a definite pattern in those countries still in process of transition. This 'eclecticism' is to be understood as an attempt to bring about what may be called a new 'synthesis of culture' by renovating their own traditional value system and combining it with the values of foreign culture. A new political system in Asia should not always be just a simple copy of the Western political one. There should be some searching for a new form that differs from both Western and indigenous forms. Although difficult, efforts in this direction have already started. To take an example we might call attention to the ideologies of 'Guided Democracy' and *Socialisme à la Indonesia* advocated by Sukarno in Indonesia. Regardless of whether it is realistic or unrealistic, *Konsepsi Sukarno* attempts to create a new form of democracy based on a democratic and co-operative spirit and way of life that is indigenously Indonesian and can be seen in the villages in Java, where any dispute among people is settled by means of *musjawarat* and *mufakat,* or unanimous consent by free talking. Sukarno insists that such a traditional democratic institution should be applied to modern national politics. Naturally, there must be great practical difficulties in extending this political institution from the village level to the national level. Furthermore, there are other difficulties involved in the concept of 'guided democracy' in the sense of how the concept of guidance will theoretically be reconciled with that of democracy. Nevertheless, it should be clearly noted that Sukarno intends to achieve a synthesis between Western political institutions and the political ideas and institutions of the Indonesian political tradition. It would not be proper to condemn Sukarnoism as mere dictatorship or a disguised Oriental despotism. But still, it is doubtful whether Sukarnoism will ever lead to a new cultural synthesis. It is my opinion that it should properly be understood as the 'eclecticism' that emerges in transitional societies. In general, I feel it is premature rather than wrong to make any definite assessment of the pattern of political acculturation of Asian countries in transition.

"In view of my examination of theories of civilizations, it should be particularly emphasized that any transmitted political and cultural values, with the exception of technology and science, will remain an *imitation deformé* and will be unable to fulfill socially productive functions unless the transmitted values are imbued with the style of the receiving indigenous culture and hence endowed with a dynamic creativity from within."

One of Itagaki's central theses was that Japanese development was helped because of its pattern of relationships with the rest of the world in the style of what he called "soil improvement," or what Mazrui dryly characterized as "casting Western manure, as it were, on Japanese soil." Itagaki had taken great pains in his presentation to point out that Japanese international relations had been of such a nature as to preclude simple comparison with the present situation or developmental prospects of such Asian countries as Indonesia or Burma. But at one level of generalization he was anxious to draw out the

Japanese experience. He saw political democracy in Japan as the outcome of a long process of economic development with some ancillary social developmental consequences. This commonly held view was shared by many around the table and was given strong support by Borsa in his later analysis of the political histories of India, Japan, and China. The presumption was also tacitly accepted that Western European cultural history shows the same relationship between the emergence of democratic institutions and preceding socio-economic changes. In retrospect, it was probably a mistake to let this casual analysis go unchallenged. Democracy or, more pertinently, political freedom and its relationship to development was of central concern in the building of the agenda. And yet it was the one important theme never developed with any richness. Attempts to introduce the subject into the debate on Itagaki's presentation consistently foundered before the greater interest in posing practical questions concerning how Japan "had been able to do it," how it had managed to modernize.

Farmanfarmaian set the tone by asking how the land reform program carried out under General MacArthur had been blended with the pre-existing land system. Both Itagaki and Gallagher pointed out that the land reform program did not and was not designed to raise agricultural productivity. The efficiency of land utilization was already very high because of reforms undertaken in the Japanese feudal period, the pressure of World War II, and the attitudes of the landlords. The land reform was, then, essentially a political operation. The civic nature of the reform was underscored by the procedures used for the distribution, which rested upon village committees deciding on how to parcel out the land in lots of no more than two hectares to the landless and the tenant farmers.

At this point Reissman stepped in to argue that land reform is often a culturally backward movement. Not only is it sometimes economically irrational to distribute small pieces of land, but also such procedures do not contribute to the formation of the class structure adequate for development along lines of national integration. In a letter to Silvert after the conference Reissman expanded this point, relating it to our failure to work the freedom problem with greater care.

"The one subject we put off throughout the conference was that concerning freedom. You had mentioned it at the opening session and after that point references were made to the subject without any concerted or sustained analysis. This was unfortunate . . . Indeed, the only one who was consistently exercised about the matter of freedom . . . was Ibish. Leaving that personalistic dimension of freedom [the possibility of maintaining certain traditional personal styles in a modern setting] aside for the moment, let me make a few points for your consideration. First, I think it should be made clear that urbanization and secularization have come to mean relatively greater freedom—and predominantly for the rural peasantry. This was certainly true in the history of the West and I gather is true in today's developing countries as well. It is not that the peasantry seeks such freedom, but that it becomes the willy-nilly recipient of it in the course of development. Secondly, it must also be stated that freedom in the full sense of the word as we understand it is at best a long-range consequence: that is, it is the presumed result of a completely successful development process. Finally, the real issue, of course, is what happens to freedom in the transition process. A rather interesting conclusion is reached by La Palombara in his essay which is part of a volume called *Bureaucracy and Political Development* [Princeton: Princeton University Press, 1963]. He says, 'One of the great dilemmas of many of the developing countries is that they seem to want economic development more than freedom.' I tend to agree.

"The validity of the conclusion goes back to the old problem of the elite. For the elite the more or less material stakes of successful economic development and greater status and power in the system override their concern with political freedom as a general democratic principle. They really don't care for anyone else. From the other side, the urban proletariat and the rural peasantry in a sense stand outside the issue of freedom. By this I mean that these latter two groups are much more interested in materialistic gains; *i.e.*, land reform, higher wages, etc., than they are interested in the more nebulous and abstract principles of freedom. I have little doubt that they know what political tyranny and political dictatorship can be, but it seems that their answer lies in increasing their material position rather than in trying to change their position vis-à-vis political roles or anything like that. Furthermore, where the tradition of society has been that of a landed feudalism or the tight control of rural villages, then there has been no experience with democracy and little aspiration for such freedom.

"I am not fully convinced that my explanation makes sense, but the important thing to remember is that very few countries are attempting to achieve development via a democratic set of alternatives. Indeed, it is my impression that the only ones who worry about freedom or the lack of it in the developing countries are the intellectuals, either the indigenous intellectuals or those from the outside. For the elites, on the other hand, freedom becomes a valid alternative only when they see it as necessary to achieve their goals—such as is the case for the English bourgeoisie in the seventeenth and early eighteenth centuries. I think the same thing can be said once again today."

These second thoughts by Reissman are quoted here to reveal what was implicit to many of the arguments concerning land reform. Farmanfarmaian, for instance, in answering Reissman's reference to the possible economic inefficacy of land reform programs, sustained that the motivation is always political and that it is impossible to await rational economic prescriptions—they take too long. He said that in Iran some groups argue that all that is necessary to maintain efficiency through land reform is to replace the unifying and controlling authority of the landlord with a co-operative. Whatever efficiency there was before will be maintained with the major difference that individuals will now be free. But the co-operatives so far established have almost all failed. The will and the organizing capacity needed to make them successful simply cannot come from the peasantry, and local government is insufficiently organized to substitute in any measure for the landlord. About half of Iran's 60,000 villages are under the agrarian law, accoring to Farmanfarmaian. "Let's assume," he said, "that we set up one co-operative for each five or six villages. That would mean we would need at least six thousand individuals who know something of double-entry bookkeeping and accounting. And you won't find five hundred accountants if you put together all the accountants in all of Iran's banks."

Farmanfarmaian continued his argument by proposing that a protected laissez-faire system could act to make farmers more participant, more of a rural middle class. So long as the government would prevent the small farmer from being gobbled up, but still leave him otherwise alone, a natural tendency toward co-operation would arise under the pressure of circumstances. But governments undertaking land reform for political reasons cannot allow the development of collective action which may later be turned against them.

The land-reform discussion then zigzagged back and forth without the central problem ever becoming the subject of clear confrontation: does land reform imply merely change or specifically that change which conduces to further development? Can land reform inhibit modernization? Silvert and Reissman argued that an independent peasantry is certainly humanly more desirable than serfdom, but that, as Reissman's letter stated, it is not necessarily that kind of change which creates a modern social structure and modern social attitudes. Apter at one point took those views to imply that large-scale farm units were being proposed as indicative of modernity. Mazrui argued that "individualization of landownership can by no means be regarded as a step backward in social organization and political integration." Apter returned to the attack with examples from Czechoslovakia, Poland, Senegal, and Mali, emphasizing the political factor in land reform in Africa. "In Mali, for example, l'Office du Niger has been nationalized and the old bureaucratic apparatus not only has changed, but it *feels* more modern. It helps to universalize a wide range of experience which previously remained remote for the farmer. The political factor has changed the meaning of the work relationship and thus the sense of discipline and the will to cooperate. The question is how long the political factor can remain the only source of motivation."

We finally left this long digression into land reform to return to Japan with Farmanfarmaian's question to Itagaki, "How were you able to succeed in having economic development without shattering traditional institutions and structures?" Itagaki responded, "We retained the ascription variable and only that one. For the rest, the movement was toward modern pattern-variables." What Itagaki was referring to, in the terminology of Talcott Parsons, was that the Japanese managed to retain consistency in the social order by maintaining a system of rewards according to the social position of the individual. In all else much pragmatism and relativism in the making of choice was introduced into the system, permitting the flexibility required for the economic development which was begun in the eighteenth century. Gallagher added that, given this time span, social disruption could be spread over a long period. Indeed, he added, Japan has experienced its revolts and civil disturbances.

Silvert saw in the Japanese case support for the general theory of political development and nationalism he had been arguing. The traditional and authoritarian Japanese society had an upper class that was able to enlarge itself to ingest and integrate the samurai. This extension of the political system at the top was accompanied by value shifts permitting the introduction of other kinds of changes and particularly modern militarism and economic development. The economic innovations were those felt immediately further down the social ladder. But there, too, the social and political effects of the changes created severe tensions even before World War II. The necessary mobilization of a population for war and for economic change raises the question of that population's later integration into the effectively participating nation. This constant enlargement of the effective nation has continued since the war, according to report.

Itagaki closed the session by remarking that in Japan, if industrialization is to continue, the old patterns of deference and ascription must be even further broken down. The recruitment of new laborers to the labor and consuming markets must be assured. Paternalistic relations can no longer be maintained, and collective bargaining must take their place.

III. LEADERSHIP AND BUREAUCRACY

Des Alwi, out of his experience as an activist political leader in Indonesia, led an applied political discussion of internal leadership and social participation that revolved about matters of charisma and power. His opening remarks concerned Indonesian political history, with emphasis on the nationalist movement and its roots in an unsuccessful princely revolt against Dutch rule in the nineteenth century. Since the beginning of the twentieth century the nationalist movement has been divided by fundamental disagreement concerning methods, despite the agreement on ends. Some groups believed in co-operation with the colonial authorities, others in passive nonco-operation, and still others in violent opposition. If some movements, particularly those in which students were involved, pushed for education of the masses, other organizations were by and for the intellectuals alone. The Communists emerged in the early post-World War I years and were subjected to a thoroughgoing repression after their abortive revolt of 1925–26. The "Javanese mystical communism" of that movement was to undergo a change into a rather more standard international mold with the passage of time. Meanwhile, despite the care of the Dutch authorities of that time, Sukarno's independence movement was also launched in the mid-1920s.

The Dutch colonial system rested on a heavy concentration and centralization of resources in the island of Java. Although Java is the most densely populated of all the islands and contains the largest single ethnic group in Indonesia, it must depend for its economic subsistence on other, richer islands. The language is one throughout the republic, but geographical distances are so great and ethnic differentiation so profound that a true national unity seemed utopian to Des Alwi at this moment. The Dutch managed to make administrative sense out of this diversity by governing through the Indonesian aristocracy. Under the Dutch governor and his immediate agents, the resident officers, the regents (who were local princes) ruled the provinces and districts. The bureaucratic apparatus established by the Dutch has not been changed, but the personnel, of course, is now almost totally different. Practically all the aristocrats on Sumatra, for example, were either killed or otherwise rendered powerless during the revolution. But on Java many of the aristocrats joined the independence movement. The maintenance of the administrative machine, however, has not permitted the present government to re-establish full control at the village level. The Dutch and the Japanese during the wartime occupation obtained compliance with law through coercion and fear, but the Sukarno government seems unable to use even these primitive stimuli.

Des Alwi's presentation confirmed the picture of inefficacy and sloganeering commonly drawn to describe the present Indonesian political scene. The obvious question which arises is just how such a situation manages to maintain itself. Des Alwi replied by stating that the army continues to back Sukarno, even though it is increasingly difficult to control officers posted to remote locations. The villagers remain apathetic, assuming that their position is about the same, whether under Dutch, Japanese, or Sukarno rule. In addition, the Javanese support Sukarno in his campaign to crush separatist or federalizing tendencies on the outlying islands, for their own economic survival depends on the maintenance of a unitary system. Itagaki here broke in to explain that even though the Indonesian constitution of 1947 was federal in form, Sukarno turned organic law around to permit the maintenance of unitary patterns.

As the interchange proceeded, it seemed clear that Sukarno was being sustained negatively by apathy, of course, but positively by his charisma on the one hand and the army on the other. Radway expounded his understanding that the polity was really dualist, split between Sukarno and his civil political entourage on one side and the army on the other, with the latter making a somewhat deliberate attempt to sink roots into the masses. How long charismatic leadership can counterbalance military might is a moot question, of course. Mazrui, Horton, and Gallagher commented on civil-military tensions in their regions of study, with all coming to the same conclusion: only complex situations of dispersed and widely distributed interests can serve to contain military ambition.

It is worth noting that no one had advanced the thesis that the military constitute a primary force for modernization in some developing countries. This contention does not lack for supporters in the United States, especially with reference to Southeast Asia and certain Latin American countries. Silvert would not defend the point of view, but he described it so as to introduce the theme. He then went on to argue that at the very least the military do indeed constitute an important channel for acculturation, for receiving international stimuli. Modern, professionalized or semiprofessionalized military forces of necessity are engaged in international relations. Their more complex weaponry must be imported; officers and often noncommissioned officers may be trained abroad; foreign advisory missions are often employed, and the growth of complex systems of military alliances during the Cold War must also be taken into account.

Most of the discussion of the military centered about their activities in the "new states" that have won sovereignty since World War II. The usual patterning of the problem was as in the Indonesian case—the untidy power of a civilian charismatic leader of the independence revolution faced by the organized might of the general. Silvert found fault both with the category of "new nations" and with the simplification of the conditions of the clash. Almost without exception the "new old" nations of Latin America fell into disarray after gaining independence in the 1820s. In every case except in Chile and Brazil *caudillos*, Latin America's famed "men on horseback," took advantage of splits in the aristocracy to seize political power. Some were Conservative *caudillos* and others Liberal ones, but in all cases they were in alliance with certain significant sectors of the civilian elite. The crumbling of central authority and of old governmental procedures as well as *intra-class* warfare (*not* inter-class) opened up the opportunity for many aspiring persons from relatively humble origins to use the military power they had gained in the wars of independence to move into the political sphere.

The historical point Silvert was making is that today's "new nations" are not necessarily unique in their problems. The suggestion by some authors that contemporary experiences in Southeast Asia should be used to explain Latin American militarism is thus chronologically backward: it is a peculiar suggestion that the experience of a few years derived from such countries as Burma and Pakistan should serve as an explanatory device for the century and a half of civil-military strife in Latin America. Even contemporary Latin America offers some cases useful in explaining military action of recent date in such countries as Egypt. Just as Perón took power as a military man but acted as an essentially civilian leader, so has Nasser followed the same path. Indeed, it might be argued that Nasserism might more properly be called Peronism in its generic form, given the chronology of the two cases.

This discussion pushed Radway to some thoughts about civil and military bureaucracies, and in a later session he made some formal remarks about bureaucracy and modernization. Because his comments fit so well at this point, however, they will be included here in full in place of a resume of his more informal statements made during the discussion following Des Alwi's story of the Indonesian case.

"By bureaucracy," began Radway, "I understand the managerial cadres of the state, both civil and military.

"The first question, logically, is whether such cadres play an independent role in political systems. To be more precise, to what extent can they constitute an autonomous force in *any* direction—traditional, modern, etc.? To what extent, on the other hand, is the bureaucracy merely a neutral instrument of changing political masters, a faithful servant of each passing regime?

"Empirically we know that managerial cadres of the state are never wholly neutral instruments of the regime. (cf. Laski's doubts about the neutrality of the British administrative class; the notorious power of the French administrator as the governing element in an otherwise unstable polity; and the free-wheeling American bureaucrat weaving and bobbing among Congressional committees and interest groups.)

"There are also some *a priori* reasons for supposing that bureaucracy may be more powerful in underdeveloped states than in those mentioned above.

"a. Because functions are less highly specialized, public officials may also have highly important political, military, ecclesiastical, or economic roles.

"b. Because literacy and education are less widespread, the public official enjoys special advantages.

"c. Because private associations and private managerial elites are relatively dwarfed or stunted, the public official faces fewer bureaucratic rivals or critics in the private sector.

"d. Colonial administration and foreign aid programs develop bureaucratic but not political institutions.

"It should not startle us, therefore, to have Joe Farman-farmaian state that Iran 'is ruled by the King and the bureaucracy.'

"In other countries, one must admit, the civil official has far less power. This is apparently the case in Indonesia, for example, and in South Korea. But in many such cases, as though a compensatory mechanism were involved, the military bureaucracy assumes a dominant power position.

"I should very much welcome comments on this hypothesis from those who have special knowledge of Latin America,

Africa, or Japan. But let us leave the point for the moment with two final observations: (1) that the precise degree of power possessed by the managerial cadres of the state is an empirical question that can only be answered by inquiry; (2) that in a sufficiently significant number of cases their power will be great enough to warrant examination of the values or attitudes of its possessors. Their power will be great enough to make the bureaucracy an important variable in determining the quality of the social process.

"The second question, logically, is whether the bureaucracy on the whole constitutes a force for maintenance of traditional society, or whether it is a spearhead of that kind of innovation to which we give the name 'modernization.'

"Mannheim, probably generalizing from recent European experience, has stated that bureaucracy everywhere tends to be a stabilizing or conservative element in the polity. And there are surely many cases that seem to support his position. Alan Horton has spoken of the Egyptian bureaucracy, not only before 1952, but even under the Nasser regime. One can think of contemporary Portugal or of the Austrian civil service in the age of Metternich.

"There are also military cases. Latin America provides many. One thinks of the French army at the time of the Dreyfus affair, supporting ecclesiastical, hierarchical, particularistic values. One is reminded, too, of Robert E. Lee, opting for the traditional social system of his native state on the very eve of the expansion of industry in North America.

"But there are also innumerable instances in which the bureaucratic cadres stand in the forefront of the modernizers. Again one is faced with a specific empirical question: which bureaucrats, civil and military, tend to be traditionalists and under what conditions? Which tend to be modernizers? With what other variables are these stances most closely related?

Social class? Age and rank? Type of ministry? (Do Foreign Offices differ from Economic Ministries?) What is their exposure to specific foreign influences?

"There is no doubt that this last factor is of *some* consequence. There is ample testimony concerning the liberalizing influence of colonial administrators on some indigenous civil servants. Analyses of the subsequent careers of graduates of Western-controlled institutions (such as Robert College in Istanbul) would be interesting if comparisons were drawn with graduates of national universities on the one hand and on the other with those who had gone to Europe to imbibe their Mazzini, Rousseau, Mill, or Marx.

"Foreign influence has clearly had a modernizing effect on certain military cadres. The obvious case is the Turkish army in the nineteenth century. Leavenworth and Benning have turned out modern-minded soldiers (as well as some highly reactionary military dictators). Historically perhaps the most important case is that of the modernizing Napoleonic armies. Those who recall only the reactionary French military of 1900 need to be reminded that one hundred years earlier this army —in which 'every soldier carries a marshal's baton in his knapsack'—struck terror into the hearts of the legitimate princes of Europe, who recognized it for the instrument of revolutionary change that in fact it was.

"What can safely be concluded? In societies in which the forces of modernization are at work the bureaucracy will be among those forces in a significant number of cases; sometimes it will be the civil bureaucracy that serves as a prime carrier of modernization, and sometimes the military.

"To the extent that bureaucracies are prime carriers, it now becomes necessary to examine their possible contributions or functions more closely. As a preliminary to such examination let me suggest that co-operative enterprises, including the state itself, may be the locus of two analytically distinct although closely interrelated sets of activities:

"1. Activities that aim at achieving the goals or purposes for which the system came into existence; e.g., to make steel, to educate children, to care for the sick, to protect the citizenry. I shall call these 'goal-achievement' activities.

"2. Activities that aim at maintenance of the enterprise itself—its internal cohesion, morale, the incentive of its members, their devotion, loyalty. I shall call these 'system-maintenance' activities. In the case of political systems the relationship to nationalism is evident.

"To repeat, the two sets of activities are closely interrelated. For example, failure to perform either set jeopardizes success in the other set and jeopardizes the future of the system as a whole. Where internal cohesion and support are absent, the system will not possess the power to grapple with its primary goals. Conversely, if over a long period of time it is unable to achieve its goals effectively, participants in the system will ultimately withdraw their support; they will cease to identify. In the case of a polity a revolutionary crisis will be at hand.

"We seem to have had examples of each of these cases at this conference. The Indonesian example appears to be one in which the technical economic tasks (goal achievement) have been subordinated so drastically to the political tasks (system maintenance) that the system may well founder. Even if it does not actually founder, a price will have to be paid for the *unevenness* of the modernization process. At the other extreme there appear to be countries which have made a good start on goal achievement; they exhibit many of the material indicators of modernization. But they have failed to generate really massive internal membership or participation in the polity. They have neglected the system-maintenance function. And this has set a fairly rigid upper limit on their continued *economic* development. If I understand correctly, this has been the predicament of Argentina.

"What has all this got to do with bureaucracy? I suggest, first, that a modernizing bureaucracy may contribute to both sets of activities—goal achievement and system maintenance.

"It will obviously contribute to system maintenance (or even system building) if it includes the equivalent of what Russians call 'agit-prop' types. It will also contribute if it opens its ranks to all social classes instead of remaining a citadel of privilege. (To this extent, incidentally, certain 'spoils systems,' such as the Jacksonian, may actually be more appropriate than merit systems during early stages of modernization; even though counterproductive from the standpoint of goal achievement, they may be highly useful for system building.) Finally, the mere existence of the public cadres serves to symbolize the nation, its unity and integrity as an entity that transcends class, regional, tribal, ethnic, religious, and other groups. This is especially true of military bureaucracies because of their obvious relation to the sovereign function of defense. In the eyes of new states a national army ranks symbolically with an airline.

"Nevertheless, I am tempted to advance the proposition that in most cases the more important contribution of bureaucracy will be toward goal-achievement activities. I invite your testimony regarding your own areas. Do not the more obvious political agencies (charismatic leadership, mass parties, etc.) play the larger role in system building and system maintenance, while the managerial cadres play the larger role in goal achievement?

"In European experience goal achievement meant the creation of a whole category of services or functions that were performed in a *public* rather than *private* manner. Functions formerly patrimonial, ecclesiastical, or dynastic were placed on a broader basis.

"1. The administration of law and justice. Crime, which at one time was a matter for private vengeance, became a breach of the public peace. Therefore it is not Richard Roe vs. John Doe, but the People of the State of New York vs. John Doe.

"2. Public finance. Taxes, at one time collected by middlemen who expected to make a profit, became collected by public officials. The personal accounts of the king were separated from the public accounts of the state. (In England this did not occur until the nineteenth century!) His love letters are separated from the national archives and his jewels from the public treasury.

"3. Defense was once a function of private armies, hired mercenaries, or middlemen. (In the U.S. in 1776 a man who raised, equipped, and fed ninety soldiers received a captain's commission; 900 soldiers were worth a colonel's commission.)

"4. Office is no longer a species of private property but a public trust. The first principle of the modern law of public administration is that no man has a contractual right in a public office.

"Both of the words we use to describe a true polity are derived, significantly enough, from Anglo-Saxon or Latin terms that suggest its distinctively public nature: commonweal and republic (*res publica;* and following Cicero, *res publica, res populi*).

"Now, to carve out a distinctly public sphere—a range of functions many of which were previously performed by less-than-public personnel—to carve this out is not an easy job. Resistance is encountered, and opposition and hostility, because power and prestige are transferred from some people to other people in the process.

"Moreover, the bureaucracy, especially in the twentieth century, is also asked to impose social discipline—the social discipline needed to decrease personal consumption so that capital can be accumulated.

"It is the fashion of our time to articulate grandiose economic goals. Once this is done the planners immediately begin to worry about obstacles to the achievement of those goals; obviously the most important of these obstacles are always found to be human. Souls can never be transformed as rapidly as things. So the minds of the planners quickly jump to the centralization and coercion needed to overcome those obstacles.

"Bureaucracy is the instrument by which taxes are levied, imports curtailed, heavy investment planned, men are drafted into the army or into labor battalions, people are transplanted, farms collectivized, strategic hamlets built. All such measures can arouse the opposition not of the traditional elites alone but, unless the country is kept in a high state of intoxication by charismatic leadership, of the masses.

"This is why modernizing bureaucracies find themselves invoking repressive, coercive, or even punitive measures to overcome resistance to their goal-achievement activities. This is why Machiavelli advised that the founders of new states had to be tough and ruthless, combining the strength of the lion with the cunning of the fox.

"But I suggest that somewhere during the modernization process—at a point that cannot be identified very precisely, and that almost surely varies from one state to another—somewhere in the process comes a time when it becomes positively harmful or obstructive to continue to press a monistic or absolutist position. There comes a time for a kind of Thermidor, for a relaxation, an about-face from earlier postures.

"1. Instead of centralization, there arises a requirement for the kind of decentralization that Charles Gallagher encountered in Tunisia—a need to restore some semblance of the autonomy that was formerly an impediment. Riggs, for example, has suggested that bureaucracy can facilitate this decentralization if it restores limited financial powers (taxing powers) to local authorities and provides for direct election of local officials. [Fred Riggs is Professor of Political Science at Indiana University, a well-known scholar in comparative public administration.]

"2. Where formerly business classes were perceived as threats to political integrity and unity because they may have been dominated by foreign capital or by ethnic and racial minorities, now there occurs a need to foster and protect a private sector, preferably dominated by entrepreneurs of native majority stock. Here again the bureaucracy may find wide latitude in shaping this occurrence.

"3. In religious affairs, where once it was essential to assert the primacy of the state over religious leaders with the secular influence or pretensions of an Innocent III or a Boniface VIII, now it becomes necessary to concede liberty and autonomy to the church so that believers may find it a refuge or protective sheath, to use Ibish's construction.

"4. More generally, where lesser associations were formerly perceived as worms within the entrails of the body politic, they must now be fostered and cherished. Bureaucracy can make at least a negative contribution to this task of pluralism by refraining from the temptation to make its work easier by creating what are in effect 'company unions,' mere appendages to its own departments and agencies that act not as independent critics but as mere transmission belts in such fields as labor, education, business, and agriculture.

"In short, at one stage bureaucracy must generate the concept of public by withdrawing functions from private hands. At a later stage it must sustain the concept of public by preventing it from devouring the entire private sector and thus, again, obliterating the distinction between public and private.

"Will it be possible for bureaucracies to make such a shift? What variables will affect its abilities to do so? Although the so-called 'objective situation'—the state of the economy, the capabilities of the population, the external or foreign situation, etc. —although these so-called 'objective' factors obviously have some bearing on whether it is possible to make the kind of a shift I have been talking about, I think it would be a mistake to take too mechanistic or deterministic, too Marxist a position on this question.

"Accidents of leadership will also have a bearing. And the ethos or values of the bureaucracy itself will be an important variable.

"This last, may I say in conclusion, is not a wholly reassuring factor. It tends to be characteristic of bureaucracies, and I suspect especially in newly independent nations, to affect the Platonic role: they are the self-appointed Guardians who have seen the Sun; they are the custodians of the 'real will' of society, and as such feel justified in forcing men to be free. Such attitudes are not conducive to that ultimate humility which, in a developed polity, sustains at least the ideal (if not always the fact) that the bureaucracy functions as a servant of society. Instead those attitudes conduce to the bureaucratic vices of corporatism, secrecy, self-recruitment, self-protection, and above all, self-aggrandizement—with the result that bureaucrats end by becoming an overpaid, overeducated, and overstaffed elite, sucking up a disproportionate share of the talents and energies that are in any event scarce in developing societies.

"In this respect, if I may be permitted a small expression of chauvinism, and it is late enough in this conference for a little flag waving, I suspect that the bureaucracies of developing nations have more to learn from the example of the American civil service than from the civil service traditions of France or England."

This summation by Radway put the final touch to the central core of the conference, to the analysis of the actual political problems, procedures, and institutions of the developing world and their relationship to nationalism. The first part of any meeting involves a mutual feeling out, self-identification, exploration, or what we called finding common ground in titling the first section of this summary. The description of that process of finding ourselves was made as short as could be done without leaving the reader at a loss as to the basic postulates of the organizers of the conference as well as of the participants.

In this second section we have permitted ourselves a greater relaxation in the presentation of the debates, for factual information of a comparative nature was being accumulated and strength being gathered for the third order of events, the beginning of projection. Do not look for a complete cessation of descriptive analysis, for the chairmen of the last group of meetings had also to describe at leisure and some length the factual bases for their suppositions. The accent, nevertheless, will now be seen to shift once again—from conceptual frameworks and historical, institutional analysis and diagnosis to a combination of diagnosis and prediction.

CHAPTER THREE

Toward Synthesis

I. *The Nation, Science, and Technology.* How does modern scientific "style" as well as artifact affect the rate and type of change? How do empirical attitudes condition political ideology, especially the temptation to technocratic solutions of "government by technician"? What is the proper role of the scientist and the expert in the nation and in the development process? What do we know—in hard terms—about the relationship among industrial technology, urbanization, and nation-building? *Chairman: David Apter.*

J. *National Development and Freedom.* Is there a functional relationship between freedom and development? What is the role of the nation-state in this relationship, whether functional or casual? The state, decision-making, ideology, and the consolidation of interest and interest groups are all here involved. Is there a relationship between the manner of exercising choice and the self-sustaining nature of development? What are the criteria for determining whether development is self-sustaining? *Chairman: Giorgio Borsa.*

K. *Policies of Integration in the Present World Context.* The effect of the contemporary international situation on nation-building and political development. The growing unevenness of national life styles as the developed grow more developed faster than the underdeveloped emerge. Is the preceding statement as true as it seems to appear statistically, or is it that the quantitative distance may be increasing but the qualitative one narrowing? What are the effects of the Cold War? What are the effects of supranationalism, regional organization? What are the economic advantages, if any, of regionalism as opposed to autarchy among developed as well as developing lands? *Chairman: James Eayrs.*

L. *Future Research.* The specific formulation of guiding concepts for future research into the political aspects of development. How can "importance" or "significance" be defined for the purpose of choosing among alternative research subjects? Should "importance" and "significance" be guiding criteria? How can comparability be attained and significance maximized at the same time? *Chairman: Ali Mazrui.*

I. SCIENCE, TECHNOLOGY, AND IDEOLOGY

Anyone who has ever prepared a conference agenda will have a profound understanding of why diplomats find it so frustrating to organize the subject matter of international meetings. As we have already seen, our conference agenda was followed up to this point with rough fidelity even though some suggested sub-themes were neglected, others introduced, and many differing meanings attached to the general subjects. This amendment and emendation were all to the good: after all, if the agenda had been sufficiently forward-looking to embrace all possible alternatives of the discussion, why have the conference at all? Adherence to the announced topics became more general as we went along, but not less pertinent. That is, the general subjects were respected, but their development began more and more to stem from the profundity of knowledge of each participant. The "conference personality" of each individual had developed sufficiently to permit the elision of some of the formally posed questions, and the clearer emergence of intuitions mingled with professional preoccupations.

The chairmanship of Mr. Apter on the subject of the nation,

science, and technology marked an important step in this progression toward the expression of the fullness of personal commitment and professional interest and their projection into views concerning the possible future course of social events. Apter provided the transition from the previous steps in which we engaged first in finding ourselves and then in finding some order in the development process. He carried us forward to informed guesses and predictions about the future. As in the cases of Borsa, Eayrs, and Mazrui who were to follow him, Apter rooted himself in a theoretical-historical analysis before taking off for the future.

Portions of Apter's theoretical views had, of course, been presented long before his uninterrupted statement, which he made turn on the questions of the ideologies of nationalism, socialism, and the social sciences as his way of inviting us to grapple with the agenda title of "The Nation, Science, and Technology." The shorter statements by Apter had almost always evoked some response from Silvert, just as the latter's constructions had often stirred Apter. In these interchanges Reissman usually acted as a relativistic moderator, holding that any theory is at least somewhat nourishing as long as it permits meaningful organization of data and reasonably valid projections. It is not that Apter and Silvert were at odds, but sometimes they were surely talking past one another. The problem may well have been that each one had put his thoughts in the concrete of writing and found trouble making the other fellow's construction fit the form he had already cast. Silvert was in the discomfiting position of having written both agenda and the theoretical portions of *Expectant Peoples*. He was troubled by two conflicting convictions: the commitment to what he had written, and the opposite commitments to unending self-doubt and to good taste in not forcing other people to agree with him. Apter had worked intensively along theoreti-

cally more inclusive and somewhat different lines from Silvert.
Aside from his already published work on many aspects of the
comparative politics of development, he had recently prepared
an introductory theoretical statement for a volume he is editing
entitled *Ideology and Discontent.** In addition, the University
of Chicago Press is preparing publication of his *The Politics of
Modernization.* Silvert's and Apter's sets of interests were not
so vested, however, as to disturb the meeting.

To open his remarks Apter directed himself to a definition of
ideology. There is an invidious sense of the word, of course, in
the presumption that ideology is a cloak designed to screen
reality or to conceal class interest. In a more intellectually
correct sense, ideology is properly understood as a body of
ideas derivative from such more abstract ideas as formal political philosophy. Ideology refers not to *any* ideas or ideals but
specifically to *political* ideas and ideals. It concerns not *any*
values but those specifying a given set of preferences, and not
to *any* beliefs, but rather those governing specific modes of
thought. "Because it is the link between action and fundamental belief, ideology helps to make more explicit the moral basis
of action." Political ideology as such is an application of particular moral prescriptions to collectivities; because the political
ideologist claims to find a relationship between higher human
consciousness and more evolved forms of material relationships, he presumes an ethical power for his ideas so that "by
virtue of his superior knowledge his view ought to prevail."

Ideology, Apter continued, serves two principal functions:
structurally, it is a solidarity device with which to weld persons
together, one of the ways in which legitimacy is made possible;
behaviorally, it organizes "the role personalities of the maturing individual," assisting the individual to find his identity, a
purposive behavioral pattern, a relation between his role and

* All of the following quotations are from this work.

his self-conception. These two elements in ideology—binding the community and organizing the "role personalities of the maturing individual"—come together to legitimize authority. "It is this relation to authority which gives ideology its political significance."

Apter continued with the argument that two general ideological persuasions are characteristic of today's developing areas—a dialogue between nationalism and socialism. The former tries to create and extend solidarity with an emphasis upon the uniqueness of each political unit. The ideologues of nationalism try to infuse people with a sense of immanence and with the idea of rebirth and moral regeneration. Such views are necessarily parochial. Socialism, however, is more pointedly an ideology of development and an emphasis upon technique. In the very special sense in which socialism is used today by many leaders of developing countries, it is "an ethic for a system of political discipline leading to an emphasis on 'science'—science for its own sake as a symbol of progress and as a form of political wisdom." This kind of ideology stresses roles useful in the achievement of a "workmanlike, rational society in which people lend a helping hand toward one another because they value highly the process of industrialization through community effort."

These new ideologies of socialism may have very little to say about property or religion and indeed are largely silent on the subject of class antagonism. The African variety of developmental socialism, Apter emphasized, delineates core values fitting to modernization rather than particular economic forms. "In this sense African socialism, like its counterparts in other developing areas, tends to look backward and forward at the same time. Although it may speak in the name of 'revolution,' in most cases political leaders are forced to make changes slowly by opening up the system to modernized roles. The result is that quite often what is called socialism is merely another name for nationalism."

Thus socialist ideologies are not necessarily always antagonistic to nationalistic ideologies, and of course they are often held in common by the same persons. But socialism always seeks a kind of universality, implying that solidarity is of those who share in this historical perspective instead of those who live in the same political unit. In describing the relationship between the new ideologies of socialist development and the state, Apter came very close to what Silvert had been calling "the value of national identification"—the state as ultimate arbiter of secular conflict. To the socialist, government is seen as a main source of development. "Unity, represented in national citizenship, is the critical form of allegiance with no other loyalties taking precedence over the state itself. Behind unity is the concept of society as a natural and organic body in which all the parts have an appointed function, especially those linked to the development process."

Developing countries tend to swing back and forth between nationalism and socialism, although each passage leaves the society in a different spot along the modernization continuum. Again Apter emphasized that he was using socialism and nationalism as analytical concepts only and that the two ideologies sometimes mingle. For example, "quite often nationalist movements take a leftward turn during the last phase of their struggle for independence. The 'radicalization of nationalism' results from a changed political emphasis." Because independence itself may no longer be the issue, and the change of authority may be less simple than the leaders thought it would be, the radicalization of nationalism may occur with the employment of socialism as a developmental ideology. To make clear how the oscillation between nationalism and socialism occurs, Apter drew a diagram on the blackboard. It had six boxes, three across and two down. The historical periods across the top he labeled "Dependence Period," "Independence Period," and "Post-Independence Period." And the two down he called "Nationalism" and "Socialism," each with a scale running from one to six. In the dependence period the prevalent ideologies often start as highly nationalistic some time before independence and then become mildly socialist immediately before independence. Then, early on in the independence period, high nationalistic ideological content reappears, only to swing sharply into strongly socialistic persuasions. Then, with maturity in the post-independence period, a middle range of nationalism recurs, to move finally into a zero point—the appearance of new ideological phenomena with the advent of truly modern society. The high points and the crises appear most sharply in the independence period. "Just after independence, nationalism goes through its apotheosis, and parochial and personal interest pale before the accomplishments of independence." Later, however, "the contradictions in culture, in social groups, and in solidarity and identity result in a sweeping re-evaluation of society in the name of progress. This is the high point of socialism . . . the major ideological crisis point in the political life of a country, because at this point it becomes either a militant socialist state or, employing moderately socialist ideas, turns accommodationist."

The end of the meaningfulness of nationalism and socialism as ideologies is heralded by the rise of an ideology of social science. Only in its vulgar senses does ideology disappear from the modern world. "Gone are the rather simple-minded explanatory notions of ideology (wrapped up in simplistic dogmas) which attribute behavior to an explicit motive such as wealth, or power." The new ideology retains potency, however, for it wraps the authority of politicians in a universal appeal to scientific reason. Scientists and technicians are used to legitimate political acts in such critical issues as nuclear armament and disarmament, common markets, inflation control, and so forth. Although the war pushed this ideological development, it also fits the rationalistic tradition of Western society. "The appeal to reason requires the competitive play of ideas in order to maximize complete information which leads to the correct course of action."

Ideology can take this most elaborate and complex form in highly developed communities when the following conditions exist: "(1) There is general acceptance of common membership in the society so that nationalism has become internalized and implicit. (2) Sufficient development has already occurred so that social dislocation requires fine adjustments rather than gross solutions. (3) Consensus prevails about which roles are functional to the continuous process of development." The problem arises, however, when these indicators of a high order of integration make possible a social science ideology which in turn tends to bifurcate the society. The scientifically trained elite, now including social scientists, in identification with policy makers constitute a new scientific establishment. They, in turn, have created a group of the disestablished—of persons once "in" or hopefully "in" who are now hopelessly "out." In Apter's words, "Modern society then is composed of a small but powerful group of intellectually participating citizens trained, educated, and sophisticated with others reduced in stature if they are scientifically illiterate."

Apter began his concluding remarks by stating that the disestablished are divided into the functionally useful persons of lower status and the redundant or functionally useless persons. The establishment and the two sections of the disestablishment have their own solidarity systems, but communications among the three are tenuous if not nonexistent. Each is a lonely group, and indeed for the functionally useless ideology seems absent and only violence a satisfying outlet. The school system in the United States manifests these new tendencies most clearly, for more and more it is dedicated to winnowing out students only on the basis of ability in order to recruit members to the new meritocracy. Nevertheless, movement up through the hierarchy is quite difficult, as can be clearly seen in the limited access of Negroes to upper reaches of the scientific establishment. Because such a system can have no really extended solidarity system, ideology is often pressed into service as an imitation of one, sometimes veering toward nationalism and sometimes toward socialism. Apter suggested that the great danger lies in a synthesis of the two ideological currents in the construction of a form of national socialism, a new applied ideology of the scientific establishment. He placed his hope in more and better and more pointed social science, arguing that "the only antidote for it is more of it, but addressed to solidarity and identity problems." All societies need to accept the openness of spirit and attitudes involved in probing "the innermost secrets of social and political life." And then an educational process which contributes to the early development of an attitude of questioning in human affairs, of "attention to discovery as a means of identifying the self," will help to break down the growing split between specialist and layman.

This construction evoked strong reactions. Mazrui entered first, claiming some reservations on the basis of African nationalism. "One could indeed argue," he said, "that in Africa nationalism has so far been the universalistic force." The ethic of Western socialism can be regarded as one of an egalitarian distribution of income, while in Africa its basic ethic is one of development. But this very dedication tends to parochialism, for it leads politicians and ideologists to center their attention on the problems of one particular country. "The universaliza-

tion of socialism in Africa hasn't happened yet," Mazrui concluded. Apter replied by saying that Mazrui was telescoping
time. Of course nationalism may begin as a universalizing,
"deparochializing" force, but in its very nature—because of the
loyalty it exacts to the state—it tends to a particularizing
effect. "In many ways, too," Apter continued, "socialism is the
product of an individual's age, a phenomenon of the reaction
of one political generation to another (and political generations do not last more than five or six years in developing
countries), a reaction of youth, an alternative ideology to na-
onalism."

Ibish introduced the variable of religion as a complication in
Apter's two-way ideological analysis. Perhaps it is that Islam,
at the highest level of abstraction, is being combated by nationalism, which in turn will be supplanted by socialism. The
birth of Nasserian Arab Socialism becomes particularly interesting in this light. But perhaps, too, Islam may be used as a
force for modernization, instead of being submitted to the de-
structive pressure of other ideologies without chance for adequate defense. For example, in the traditional Muslim village
the principal legitimating agent for political processes is religion itself. Cannot nationalistic and socialistic politics be
linked to such abstractions as equalitarianism, posited as beneficial by Islam? In addition, perhaps Islam can offer some
defense against the more dangerous consequences of accepting
a social science ideology. Scientific truth is one thing, Ibish
argued, and symbolic religious truth quite another. Because
Islam has its roots in the individual, who must testify to his
belief by his life, matters of solidarity and identity can be at
least partially resolved by admitting the individual to religious
as well as scientific truth. "A Muslim remains a Muslim on a
desert island, which you cannot possibly expect a Communist
to do."

Apter rejected this possibility of religious and scientific accommodation for cultures as a whole. "The secularization process is so fundamental that the extension of the dialogue to include religious ideologies cannot work for a very long time." Individual crises may be blunted, of course, Apter pointed out, but eventually decisions concerning secular rationalization must be made in the course of development.

Apter then proceeded to give some examples of the clash between socialistic and nationalistic ideologies in Africa. He talked of Sekou Touré of Guinea, accused by socialist youth groups of betrayal because he is positing an African way to socialism and because he denies the universality of class struggle. Apter argued that the classification of identity patterns is made possible only by some such approach, for the world view of the person prototypical of one view is entirely different from the world view of the person holding the opposed one. Naturally some individuals are caught between the two. "People themselves do not have to be consistent. I am just pushing the trends to build two types."

Silvert here re-entered the discussion. It seemed to him that so long as the argument remained at the level of ideology, then there was nothing but a terminological disagreement between Apter and Silvert. But when nationalism is treated as a value of national identification, then institutional questions of great import arise. National values then funnel into consensual acceptance, creating the power of the state to do all those things which Apter says a developmental socialism must accomplish. In a way, then, as we have said, Apter's socialism has some correspondence to Silvert's values of national identification.

But still, it may be analytically useful to think of socialism as being one particular kind of national organization, instead of being opposed to it, even if merely at the ideological level and not at the value and organizational levels of things. Thus na-

tionalism can be thought of as a more generic way of organizing a community, and socialism as a more specific claim concerning the nature of organization at the instrumental level.

Silvert thus was also saying that he could accept Apter's
argument that socialistic ideology sometimes pretends to uni-
versalism but that in fact it is just as parochial as the nations
within which it develops. Marx posited an international solidarity of the working class (he may have been just extrapolat-
ing from the cosmopolitanism of the aristocracy), but in fact
no such movement has ever developed. Socialism has become
nationalized—and Silvert maintained that it was in its nature
to do so. Thus, one must take great care not to accept the self-
appreciation of ideologists, whether socialist or not, at face
value. Such information is valuable but incomplete for the
analysis of such problems as those at hand. Silvert concluded,
"I just can't imagine a socialist state which isn't national, although the reverse is often the case. So two different levels of
analytical generalization are involved if we go beyond the express opinions of the ideologues."

Eayrs broke this interchange by proceeding to the concluding part of Apter's analysis. He wanted to know to what extent
the process of the growth of a scientific establishment held true
for all the developed countries. In the United Kingdom "I
rather see what I might call an increase of the alienation of
the scientist," he said. "I wonder also whether the tension you
described in the United States is not in fact being bridged by a
new ideology in the first sense in which you used the word;
that is, a pseudo-scientific ideology of integration, a new Cape
Canaveral ideology of common participation in scientific
achievements." Apter replied that this equalitarian integration
mystique of participation in a scientific community creates "a
terrible strain, a heavy burden for those who, having this mystique, can't really achieve participation. Our problem is that

our meritocracy cannot in fact handle inequality—a growing inequality."

There were a few more comments about Apter's contentions concerning the new social science elite, and the discussion broke up for lunch. But the last remarks, appropriately from Apter, cast the discussion clearly in the careful light of Apter's analysis. His summary is worth repeating: "There is a confusion involved between the nation-state as a concrete entity and the ideology of nationalism. Most modern political systems in the developing areas try to embody both nationalism and socialism. That's why, when you distinguish between these two ideologies, you seem to be violating reality. The purpose of this separation, however, is to show a kind of ideological tension which affects the ways in which people identify themselves or feel solidarity. I do not claim anything more than that for the pair of categories I have proposed."

II. DEMOCRACY AND WESTERNIZATION

At this point we halted for stocktaking. Gallagher had prepared himself to detail the inventory, a job he carried out with punctiliousness and dispatch. He first talked about areas in which broad agreement had been reached, noting that we all saw the growth of national integration as a total social process involving economic, social, political, and ideological components. We also seemed to have found that stages in the growth of the nation do indeed exist, even though we had assigned no specific names to parts of the process. All of us also seemed certain that these stages had to be viewed as very grand categories, and that even so it now seemed possible for societies to skip from very primitive levels of organization directly into the problems of modernization. If the process is not unilineal in any narrow sense, however, it certainly does not go backward—from economic development to tribalism.

If our discussions had revealed our problems in fitting together all the elements of the national mosaic, even such a difficult subject as religion had yielded some consensus. Certainly no one had suggested a purely religious nationalism, and secularism has been viewed as at least an inevitable component of the growth of full national identification, if not a necessary element. We also tended to isolate economic matters. All the participants made a sharp distinction between economic and political development. Although this analytical technique may be but a crotchet of this particular meeting, dedicated as it was to political subjects, the reason may also be a more laudable one: that we see economic development as of primary importance but not as a criterion of national development in and of itself.

Gallagher then listed some points neglected or omitted:

1. The historical approach, and particularly the history of ideas, had been almost entirely neglected except for Itagaki's presentation. (Borsa's statement and Reissman's answer were soon to remedy this neglect.)

2. The development of nationalism in the presently industrialized countries of the West has been dealt with all too lightly. This neglect stems not only from our insufficient attention to history but also from the area interests of the participants.

3. Insufficient attention has been paid to factors of time and to rate of change. Velocity and the physical size of the societies we have been comparing have not been given sufficient attention.

4. We have also elided the problems arising from asymmetry in the development process—that is, from the twisting which always takes place when, for example, material economic development seems to outstrip the political capacity to breathe order into public affairs. Another term used to describe this phenomenon is "asynchronous" development.

5. The organization of the nation in bureaucratic and administrative terms, in an entirely practical and descriptive manner, has also been little touched on. (Radway's presentation, already included, answered this lack immediately after Gallagher finished.)

6. We have talked about large collectivities but too little about individuals and small groups. Who becomes a nationalist? How? When? What is the relationship between an individual's becoming a nationalist in a developing area and other objective and subjective data about that person?

With respect to continuing sources of disagreement among the group, Gallagher suggested three main wellsprings of argument. One, of course, was the persistent difficulty with terminology and definitions. Although tamed for the purposes of talk by greater understanding among members of the group some tension necessarily continued. Then several differences of approach still caused some misunderstanding. The historically oriented and those with a contemporary empirical approach were still sparring on some issues, as were the humanists and the social scientists. A more subtle split had also opened between those who emphasized functions and those underscoring structures. Even though structuralism and functionalism are often expounded in the same theoretical breath, functionalists like to look for social actions which describe all societies everywhere, while structuralists are much more apt to look for more specific groups of phenomena. Part of the division between economists and other social scientists can be explained in these terms, at least for those economists who assume universal principles as lying behind their science.

Gallagher concluded by describing where he would like to see the remaining sessions go. Here he limited himself to a very general remark concerning the role and place of the "new" individual in his "new society" and the place of that "new" society in the world community. Also, he asked, "can we assume that the 'new' society and the modern man are more adjusted, more integrated, and more integrative with respect to the world?" Thus, he ended, he would also like to consider the new patterns of international co-operation and association which need to emerge if the developing countries are to become full partners in the comity of nations.

Some of Gallagher's desires were to be satisfied. But others, especially those relating to more subtle matters concerning the spelling out of the possible internal patterns of developing societies, of necessity were left unanswered. A conference of this nature is simply not the place for that kind of fine tailoring. We had to content ourselves with the production of ideas and suggestions, at the same time being grateful for whatever was offered by way of specific example or hypothesis. We were fortunate in having Borsa, Eayrs, and Mazrui as the last three chairmen, for all three are inclined toward the historical approach and yet remained unafraid of the political generalization. None of them proposed any large theoretical schema, but by this time we were prepared to listen to their more detailed presentations against the backdrop of the various organizing devices already proposed.

Borsa's agenda subject concerned the question of whether there is any necessary relation—positive or negative—between freedom and development. He chose to develop this subject through a comparative analysis of India, China, and Japan and by defining freedom essentially as formal democracy. Borsa began:

"The beginning of modernization in Eastern Asia was the result of the Western impact. Not in the sense often implied by nineteenth-century European historiography, that Europeans through the medium of colonization carried modern civilization into the East—as though civilization were a fluid that can be poured from one vase into another—but in the sense that the Western economic, political, legal, and cultural impact caused (or hastened) the disruption of the traditional Asian societies, setting in motion an autonomous process of change and challenging traditional values, leading to their reappraisal. If I may use Toynbee's terminology without thus implying that I subscribe to his philosophy of history, I would say that the modernization of Eastern Asia is as much a result of the Asian response as it is of the European challenge."

Borsa then pointed out that the Western impact really began to be felt intensively after the Industrial Revolution. In the three preceding centuries the commercial contacts of Portuguese, Dutch, French, Spanish, and British merchants with the East were limited. Regularized trade was almost impossible. "If China, India, and the other Eastern countries were little affected by Western trade, not much greater was, at this stage, the influence of Western culture." He then described the ebbing of Christian influence after an initial proselytizing success and turned to the effects of Western science. "A certain influence was exerted on Eastern cultures by Western science and technology even as early as the seventeenth and eighteenth centuries, particularly in the fields of astronomy, cartography, navigation, medicine, and the use of firearms. But these innovations had little effect on Asian societies."

He continued with the thesis that "in the seventeenth and particularly the eighteenth centuries the Eastern influence on the West was altogether stronger than the Western influence on the East." Borsa suggested that this view is interesting not because it has not been advanced before, but because this interpretation seems to cast some light on the receptivity to alien cultural stimuli of traditional societies on the one hand and of those beginning the process of modernization on the other. This kind of analysis is also a partial answer to Gallagher's desire for more knowledge concerning acculturation and the growth experiences of those nations which were later to become imperialistic.

Borsa explained how the East Indian trade became a major factor not only in the British protocapitalist economy but also in British politics, provoking the most violent controversies. "The beautiful Indian cottons had become so fashionable and popular as to upset the domestic manufactures of woolens and silks. The British Parliament was urged to prohibit the use of Indian fabrics, which it did. It even passed a law ordering that corpses should be buried in woolen shrouds. Women wearing the transparent Indian muslims were accused of being immoral and for the sake of decency they were stripped of their clothes in the streets by enraged mobs of weavers in what were called 'calico chases.'" Asian crafts influence British fashion to this day; in fact, it was also about this time that the tea drinking habit spread among English-speaking peoples.

English economic thought was also affected. "The pamphleteers putting the arguments for the East India Company against the criticisms of the mercantilist school had no little influence on the author of *The Wealth of Nations*. In France the Physiocrats were influenced by Chinese thinking, and Chinese this-worldliness and Hindu tolerance were a source of inspiration to Voltaire and the other encyclopedists."

Borsa then turned to the effects of the Industrial Revolution and the imperialistic expansion that followed it, two factors that completely changed the previous relations between East and West. The following picks up and quotes directly from Borsa's statement to its completion.

"The first dramatic change occurred in the trade between Britain and India. After the monopoly of the East India Company was abolished in 1813 and trade was made free for all British merchants, British exports of cottons to India went up from 818,208 yards in 1814 to 51,737,000 yards in 1835. In the same time Indian exports declined from 1,266,000 to 306,000 yards. Five years later the East Indian Company (setting aside Sir Thomas Roe's advice which it had followed for two centuries, 'If you will profit, seek it at sea and in quiet trade') proclaimed its paramountcy over the Indian states. Similar developments occurred in other East Asia countries. The Europeans were no longer content with holding a number of trading outposts but brought vast territories under their control. These territories began to be looked upon as markets for European manufactured goods, sources of raw materials, and later as markets for capital and as balancing factors in the movement of international payments. The colonial powers forced a new economic pattern upon their dependencies and upon countries like China which remained nominally independent but were powerless to resist encroachment from the West. An economy that had largely been an agricultural, subsistence economy, centered on the self-sufficient village, began to give way to an economy in which the production of raw materials and cash crops for export acquired a growing importance. In some dependencies this was accompanied by the painful consequences of the introduction of alien legal concepts. In India, for instance, the recognition by the British of individual ownership of the land in place of a stable, customary possession by the village community brought with it contract law, mortgage, distraint, and forced sales. Where the zamindari system prevailed, the so-called "sunset law"—that is, a law introduced by the British that provided for seizure and forced sale of the land if the land tax had not been paid by sunset of the prescribed day—caused the land to change hands in the space of one generation from the old zamindaris into a new class of absentee landlords—mostly moneylenders who were able to take advantage of the sunset law.

"In the *ryotwari* zones, the peasants, no longer protected against their poverty and their extravagance by not being able to dispose of the land, lost it and became tenants and agricultural laborers. The opportunity of purchasing the land made it possible for strangers, even for town people, to intrude into the village that was once a closed community. With the commercialization of agriculture, the money economy penetrated the village. The peasants, forced by the need of cash—and by the pressure of the European planters—to turn from subsistence farming to the cultivation of cash crops, became involved in the price fluctuation of the world market, falling deeper and deeper into debt to the moneylender or to the local merchant, who acted as middleman between the peasant and the Western trading agencies. Attempts such as those made by the Dutch in Java to establish a dual economy failed. It was the very logic of colonial relationship that made the disintegration of the village economy inevitable. Village handicrafts and cottage industries, which for centuries had made the village a self-sufficient community and had provided an additional source of income to the peasants, began to be affected by the standardized, cheap goods coming in from the West. The fabric of social relations within the village based on the joint family, on caste, on exchange according to a fixed pattern of goods and services, was shattered. On top of this came an unparalleled increase in population, favored by the welfare measures introduced and by the internal peace guaranteed by Western rule, which upset the balance between land and population. Stability and security—which, though at a very low level, had been a distinguishing mark of Oriental societies—began to give way to insecurity and to change.

"The decisive factor, however, the real turning point, was the introduction of Western education and culture.

"If I were asked to pick a date from which to make modern

history start in Eastern Asia—for obviously periodization cannot be the same there as in European history—I would say 1813. In renewing for twenty years the charter of the Company that year, the British Parliament introduced in it a number of provisions that changed the course of East Asian history. First, it abolished the Company's monopoly in the Indian trade, giving it in exchange a monopoly of the trade with China. The Indian market was thus thrown open to the individual merchant, which not only altered the pattern of trade between India and Britain but also affected Indian society in the way we have already seen. On the other hand, by concentrating the Company's trading interests on China, it caused that development of the China trade that led to the Opium War and to the opening of China. And when you think that President Fillmore, in sending Perry's 'black ships' to Yedo, wanted some Japanese ports opened as a basis for American merchant vessels competing with the British in the China trade, you will see that it really all started with the Charter Act of 1813.

"This Act included three other momentous provisions: (1) it definitely asserted the sovereignty of the Crown over the territories administered by the Company and therefore its moral responsibility for the Company's subjects; (2) it lifted the ban on the establishment of the Christian missions in British India; (3) it provided for the Company's setting aside an annual sum of 1 lac of rupees (100,000 r.) for the promotion of learning among the people of India.

"The controversy which followed between the so-called *Orientalists* and the *Anglicists* on what sort of learning was to be promoted ended with the full-fledged victory of the Anglicists. The Anglicists were the sons of their time, that is, the time of Positivist Enlightenment. They felt in the words of Macaulay's famous minute on education—that 'all the historical information which has been collected from all the books written in the

Sanskrit language is less valuable than what may be found in the most paltry abridgments used at preparatory schools in England' and that it would be folly to countenance at public expense 'medical doctrines that would disgrace an English farrier, astronomy that would move laughter in girls of an English boarding school, history abounding with kings forty feet high and reigns thirty thousand years long, and a geography made up of seas of treacle and seas of butter.' Accordingly, the Company began to set up a number of schools in which English was taught in the lower grades and Western science, history, literature, law, etc., were taught *in* English at the higher levels. The Christian missions, now free to operate, powerfully cooperated in the spread of Western education. At the same time the acceptance of ultimate responsibility for its Indian subjects by the British Crown, the growth of the Liberal Party in British politics, the moral pressure exerted by such groups as the Utilitarians (both James and John Stuart Mill were officials of the East India Company) and by the evangelicals brought about a drastic change in the Company's policy. While in the past the Company, whose object was trade, had deliberately refrained from interfering with local customs and traditions except in so far as it was necessary for the sake of trade, it was now felt that the British Crown and Parliament could no longer tolerate or, in some cases, patronize, as the Company had done, cruel or immoral practices such as thuggee—that is, religious murder or suttee, the burning of widows. Under the governorship of Lord Bentinck in the 1830s the Company embarked on a policy of sweeping reforms which aimed at a gradual Westernization and, in the hope of the evanglicals, Christianization of Indian society.

"At first it seemed as though Macaulay's proud dream of an India anglicized 'through the blessings of the European condition' might have a chance of coming true. In the space of one generation a restricted class of Western-educated Indians, accepting Western standards, Western values and Western ways of life grew up, particularly in Bengal, where they became known as the babus, but also among the Parsees and the Marathis of Bombay. But it soon became clear that if the outward forms of Western civilization could be easily copied, the spirit of that civilization would take time to assimilate. With the Bengali babus, modernization meant ritual meals of beef to symbolize the break with tradition; it meant drinking spirits, kicking aside the old morality as a set of meaningless restrictions, and taking up the free and easy ways of the West. Contrary to Macaulay's expectations, Western education could not reach beyond a tragically thin upper crust. The bulk of the people remained embedded in their old ways of living and thinking.

"The only real impact of Western thought in India at this stage was made, oddly enough, in the field of religion, with the founding of a number of reformist sects among not only Hindu but also Muslim, Jain, and Parsee groups. The most important one was the Brahmo Samaj, a theistic sect bent on purifying the Hindu religion from what were held to be later distortions and superstitions in order to restore it to its original purity, at the same time incorporating in it what was worth while from the West. Unlike the Bengali babus, the founder of the Brahmo Samaj, Ram Mohan Roy, made a real contribution and gave effective support to the policy of reform carried out under Lord Bentinck in the 1830s.

"All this, of course, could not fail to provoke a reaction. The attempts at reforming and modernizing Hindusim and the other religious faiths fostered religious revivalism by contrast among the orthodox. Other sects sprang up, aiming, like Dayananda's Arya Samaj or Ramakrishna and Vivekananda's Mission, at a full defense of the old faiths. The traditionalists were shocked and alarmed at the changes brought about in Indian society by the Feringhees. Their feelings culminated in that great unpheaval that goes under the name of Indian Mutiny. This was *not* a military revolt, as most of the British nineteenth-century historians describe it, or the first war of independence, as the Indian nationalist historians would make us believe. It was an unplanned, emotional outburst at the root of which there was the economic and social dislocation caused by the Western impact and the revulsion caused by the reformist policy pursued under Lord Bentinck in the 1830s.

"The Mutiny and its suppression by the British taught the Indians that the British raj could not be dealt with in this way. After 1860 the Indian educated class began to engage in organized political activity. It was at this stage that Indian nationalism was born.

"It was born as a twofold result of the Western impact. In the state of flux and uncertainty that was caused by the breaking down of traditional society and values, nineteenth-century European culture, with its emphasis on liberty and progress, on equality and change, awoke a political interest in the intellectual elites and made the Indians conscious of their own problems and of the possibility of solving them. At the same time, by providing a sharp contrast and by training them in historical and philological research, it made them aware of their own cultural heritage and tradition. It favored the formation of a Western educated class aiming at reshaping Indian society along Western lines, and it caused a revulsion among the traditionalists leading to a new appreciation of traditional values and to a religious and cultural revivalism. From the beginning, Indian and, as we shall see, Asian nationalism had two souls and developed as a result of an inner tension, sometimes of a clash, between two opposite trends, lying beneath and coming to the surface in turn: one was progressive, Western-orientated, open to new values, secular in outlook; the other was conservative, inclined to challenge Western values, inward-looking, often pervaded with a deep religious strain. When on the first day of our discussions I listened to Professor Ibish and Mr. Farmanfarmaian arguing across the conference table about modernization and tradition, I could not help feeling that I was watching two very refined, intellectually mature incarnations of these two souls.

"In India the first flush of Western imitation brought about, as a reaction, the Mutiny. This was followed by almost half a century in which the Indian political scene was dominated by Western-educated and Westward-looking liberals, like a Daddabhai Naoroji, a G. K. Gokhale, a Surrendranath Bannerjee, a Justice Ranade, etc. It was these men who, together with a few enlightened Englishmen, founded the Congress in 1855 and led it for almost twenty years. But at the turn of the century a new militant nationalism emerged, influenced on one hand by the Western Anarchist and Nihilist movements and on the other by the religious revivalism of the Ramakrishna Mission. For the first time a terrorist movement developed in India, and new men like B. G. Tilak, Aurobindo Gosh, Bipin Chandra Pal captured, just before the First World War, the Congress leadership. They had a new concept of nationalism. It was no longer the liberal concept of a striving for national unity, freedom, and representative institutions. It became a religion, the cult of Mother India identified with the Goddess Khali.

" 'What is nationalism?' wrote Aurobindo Gosh. 'It is not a mere political programme; it is a religion, that has come from God; it is a creed you shall have to live. . . . The work of national emancipation is a ritual sacrifice . . . liberty is the fruit we seek from the sacrifice and the Motherland the Goddess to whom we offer it.'

"This religious strain is of course a major factor in Gandhi's

nationalism, which had a decidedly revivalist character and a
marked anti-Western bias, with its outright rejection of the
'monster God of materialism' under which the Western nations
were 'groaning.' But again Gandhi's back-to-the-village, spin-
ning wheel–addicted, fasting and ahimsa-practicing neo-Hin-
duism was superseded after the mid-1930s by Nehru's secularism and socialist democracy and by Patel's practical, organizational empiricism.

"And now turning to Japan, insularity is believed to have
favored an early development of a natural consciousness in
that country. Signs of it appear as early as the twelfth century
at the time of the unsuccessful Mongol invasion in the
Kamakura era. Contacts with the Europeans in the sixteenth
century and the policy of seclusion that followed, by emphasizing Japan's cultural and political distinctiveness, may have
contributed to a further development, and this may have also
come about as a natural reaction to the long-standing Chinese
cultural dominance. But the two major factors were: (1) the
crisis of feudal society under the Tokugawa; and (2) the
shock caused by the Opium War, by the fear of Russian designs over the northern part of the archipelago, and by the
arrival of Perry's black ships in the Bay of Yedo.

"Much the same as in Europe, the development of national
consciousness in Tokugawa Japan was associated with the final
overthrow of feudalism. As in Europe, this came about
through the restoration of the authority and power of the monarchy. But while in Europe, particularly in France, it was the
monarchy that took the lead in the anti feudal struggle, in
Japan a coalition of disgruntled samurai, of big Tokugawa
merchants, and of frustrated court nobles used the imperial
line as a national symbol to overthrow the Tokugawa shogun-
ate.

"This is what gave Japanese nationalism from the beginning

a distinctively revivalist flavor that could go along with the acceptance of modern technology, science, and so forth. For the ideological basis of the Meiji restoration was twofold: it rested on one hand on the Kokugaku or 'National Learning' school that conceived the overthrow of Tokugawa feudalism in terms of a restoration—that is, of going back to the prefeudal days of Japan's history, when both the sacral and political power resided with the Emperor, the direct descendant of the Sun Goddess of the Yamato clan and of the Supreme Shinto Priest. On the other hand, it also rested on the Rangaku or Dutch Learning School. This had been developed in the eighteenth and nineteenth centuries by a small but intellectually vigorous band of students who, working through the medium of the Dutch language which they learned amid great difficulties from the interpreters of the Dutch settlement in Nagasaki Bay, pursued with undaunted perseverance the study of European sciences, particularly medicine, mathematics, astronomy, and physics. It is from this group that such men came as Sugita Kempaku and Fukuzawa Yuchichi, the founder of Keio University, who favored a complete renovation and integration of national life and society through a system of education based on Western civilization and science.

"Here again you find from the very beginning this polarization between tradition and modernization. And this becomes again the central motif in the development of Japanese nationalism. For the fifteen years that followed the arrival of Perry's black ships at Yedo Bay one July morning of 1853, the issue is blurred and confused. A struggle developed between two parties. One, the *Jo-i, or* 'Expel the Barbarians' party, led by the Lord of Mito and backed by the Kyoto Court and the majority of the feudal lords, maintained that the requests made by Perry and subsequently by Townsend Harris should be rejected and the barbarians dealt with in the traditional way—

that is, thrown out. The other party supported the shogun's policy of *Kaikoku* or 'opening the country.' This party, however, was divided; the majority of its supporters and the shogun himself hated the barbarians but were realistic. They had been made aware of the barbarians' strength by the Chinese Opium War and they were in favor of giving in, only to gain a respite and to strengthen their defense by learning the barbarians' military technique and to get their weapons. Only a few, representing the progressive wing, were in favor of *Kaikoku* because they thought that trade with the Western countries and the adoption of Western capitalism was the only way out of the economic structural crisis and social strains that had marked the second half of the Tokugawa era.

"Oddly enough, it was the thesis of this minority that prevailed in the end. Still more oddly, their policies were carried out after the overthrow of the Tokugawa by those same members of the *Jo-i* or 'Expel the Barbarians' party who, after the restoration, formed the Meiji oligarchy. And it was the former *Jo-i* who, after the overthrow of the Tokugawa, crushed the attempt made by a Satsuma samurai to put the clock back and restore feudalism.

"The answer the historians give to this apparent contradiction is that the cry *Jo-i* was largely used as a means to bolster the morale of the samurai by appealing to their nationalistic feelings and as a stick to beat the shogun, who was forced to give in to the barbarians. Nevertheless, the existence of feudalism in Japan, as in Europe, had paradoxically favored the development within the feudal system and beneath the upper feudal crust of a commercial protocapitalist economy and of a prosperous merchant class of *chonin* or burghers that would have made the preservation of the policy of seclusion suicidal, for the feudal agrarian economy on which this structure rested had long been superseded by a protocapitalist economy that was open to integration with the Western economy.

"The dialectics of Western-oriented, progressive *versus* conservative, inward-looking nationalism did not end, however, with the opening of the country and the acceptance of the principle of modernization by the Meiji leaders. For their program of modernization included the development of a capitalist system, industrialization, Western science and technology, centralization of power, and modernization of the armed forces, but it did not include Western values and Western nineteenth-century liberalism. As we have seen, it rested on the *Kaikoku* ideology. The Meiji oligarchy remained opposed to popular control of government.

"A new tension thus developed between the Meiji oligarchy and what were the ideal heirs of the *rangaku* scholars, who now favored modernization and Westernization also of political institutions. The usual polarization took first the form of a conflict between a democratic movement started by Itagaki and supported by such writers as Nakae Chomin and Veki Emori, influenced by the French encyclopedists, Mill, Bentham, and so forth, and the Meiji oligarchy, that opposed the constitutional ideal. After the very conservative, German-inspired Meiji constitution was granted in 1889, the struggle went on between the newly formed political parties—that is, the supporters of parliamentary rule and the military-bureaucrat-big merchant coalition which, led by the *Genro*, continued to use the mystic quality of the Emperor as a sham behind which they exerted unrestrained power. After the First World War it seemed possible for a while that the parliamentary forces might assert themselves, but in the 1930s, for a number of internal and external causes, they were again defeated, submerged by the new wave of revivalist, militant, reactionary nationalism that goes under the name of Japanese Fascism.

"For what reasons China should have reacted so differently from Japan to the brusque contact with modern Western civilization is, to the historian, a fascinating problem. The answer for the historian, of course, lies in China's different past and the different state of Chinese society when the Europeans forced it open.

"China had already passed the feudal stage when the Christian era began and had slowly developed a highly centralized bureaucratic state and a society whose backbone had become, by the time of the Sung (960–1126), a gentry class which combined economic and political power with the monopoly of culture. Though they usually lived in the district, prefecture, and provincial towns, the members of this class owned most of the land and found in usury and trade a supplementary source of wealth. From its ranks came most of the scholar-administrators, a fact which also gave them political power and the monopoly of education.

"The commercial revolution that marked the transition from classical to premodern China, reaching its peak between the late T'ang and the Southern Sung (750–1279), could thus be absorbed and digested by the existing political and social structure. The lack of any rigid class distinction such as is found in feudal societies, the fact that the Chinese state and its scholar-administrators had been engaged from the time of the Han in economic entrepreneurial activities through the state monopolies, and the comparatively advanced stage already reached by Chinese science, technology, and economic organization made it possible for the Chinese state and society not only to adjust to the change brought by the commercial revolution but actually to draw new strength from it. The growth of commerce and the expansion of the money economy did not lead as in the West and in Japan to the formation of a mer-

chant or bourgeois class that, finding itself in conflict with the
feudal political and economic setting, had to break completely
away from it to develop or even to survive. It was this
estrangement and this break that made further modernization
possible in Europe and Japan after the commercial revolution.
In China the merchant could always invest and tended to invest his money in land which gave him social status and made
him part of the ruling class. He could fit into the existing system; the establishment was open to him. Thus the flexibility of
Chinese society and the strength of the Chinese monolithic
state combined in making the process of modernization in
China a truncated development.

"By the time of the Southern Sung (1127–1279) Chinese
society had reached a high degree of development and stability and there were few further stimuli to change. Neo-Confu-
cianism—as systematized under the Southern Sung by Chu
Hsi, with its identification of moral and social laws with the
natural law—had definitely turned Confucianism, which with
Confucious himself had revolutionary or at least reformist implications, into a doctrine of pure conservativism.

"This stability of Chinese society must no doubt have been a
great blessing for those who lived in it. Certainly life must
have been more enjoyable than in the turmoil of European
history from the Renaissance onward through the religious and
dynastic wars, English and French revolutions, and Napoleonic Wars. But this very perfection and stability also caused
Chinese society and culture to become stiff, almost ossified.
When in the middle of the nineteenth century the brusque
contact with the dynamic civilization of the West posed difficult problems of adjustment, it was utterly unprepared and
unable to cope with them.

"These pale, red-haired devils with the long noses were difficult to handle. They wanted to trade, but they refused the only

proper, time-honored way of doing so that consisted in bringing goods to the Emperor as tribute and receiving in exchange
the presents that in his Confucian benevolence he would give
back. Moreover, the Opium War, or, as they called it, 'the Barbarian Incident,' had shown that the black ships could do a
lot of harm.

"For twenty years, between the Opium War and the Arrow
War, the rulers of China deluded themselves into thinking that
they would be able to control the new barbarians from across
the sea by the same methods used by their progenitors against
the barbarians from the steppe. As the Great Wall was no use
against the seafaring barbarians, a movement first developed
for building up coastal and maritime defense. Attempts were
made to play the European powers one against the other as
the Ming had done with the Mongol and Turched tribes.
When these measures, too, proved inadequate, a policy of con-
ciliation was tried, substituting what were called 'skillful methods' and were, in fact, appeasement for force. This was still
in the tradition. Had not the Sung emperors bought off the
Liaos and the Chins by paying tribute to them? Meanwhile efforts could be concentrated on quelling the Taiping
rebellion with its dangerous Christian and modernizing implications.

"After the Arrow War it became evident that the barbarians
could not be handled this way. A new theory emerged that
called for 'self-strengthening through the adoption of Western
knowledge and the manufacture of foreign weapons and
ships.' The first arsenals and shipyards were established in the
1850s and 1860s and efforts were made to learn Western military strategy and drilling. When the first railway, built by a
British merchant company, was bought and destroyed by the
Chinese government, after it had been ascertained that the air
became poisoned, that grazing cattle were startled, and that

hens would lay no more because of it, Tseng Kuo-fang started a movement in favor of 'building railways for strategic purposes.'

"This attitude rested on the assumption that Western technology was a sort of ability or skill that had no intimate relation to Western culture and could be acquired by the Chinese without their traditional values and outlook being affected. This attitude was expressed in the neo-Confucian formula: Chinese learning and values as Ti or substance, and barbarian learning as Yung or function, that is 'for practical purposes.'

"It took some time before the doubt began to creep in that there might be something more behind Western technology. A Chinese journalist, Wang-tao, who spent two years studying in the British Isles around 1870, was the first to note, in coming back, that British power did not rest on steamships and firearms alone but also on 'a sympathetic understanding between the governing and the governed, on a close relationship between the rulers and the people.' Some years later the first translations of John Stuart Mill, Spencer, Darwin, Huxley, Adam Smith, and so forth, began to appear. They were by a student of the Foochow naval school who had spent several years in Britain for training—Yen Fu.

"Yen Fu had an important influence on later Chinese intellectuals including Mao Tse-tung, who acknowledged it. He certainly had a great influence on the leaders of the 100 Days of Reform Movement in 1898, Liang Ch'i-ch'ao and K'ang Yu-wei. The latter, a frustrated mandarin of low grade, had come into prominence by securing the signature of some 1300 candidates in the Imperial Examinations to a memorial known as the 'Letter of Ten Thousand Words,' in which the Emperor was urged to adopt a series of reforms. The young Emperor, Kwang Hsu, appointed him to an important ministerial post and on his advice issued in a little over three months a number

of decrees introducing Western reforms in various fields from
the promotion of scientific studies and the adoption of Western
military drills to the promulgation of a public budget, modernization of education and agriculture, and so forth. The
reformists, however, were ideologists without either political
experience or a knowledge of existing economic and social conditions. Before the reforms could have any effect, they had
evoked a strong opposition from the conservatives. With their
backing the Empress Dowager resumed the regency, impris-
oned the Emperor, and reversed the pro-Western policy of
reform. In order to protect the dynasty the conservatives encouraged the mounting xenophobia, making the 'white devils'
responsible for all the difficulties that Chinese society was ex-
periencing and that were the result of its inability to adjust to
the new conditions. The rising nationalist feeling was given a
violent, reactionary twist that exploded two years later in the
Boxer Rebellion and war. The Boxer uprising holds in the
history of modern China the same place as the Mutiny does in
the Indian history; it was the effect of much the same causes
and had much the same results. Like the Mutiny in India, it
was followed by the same dialectical contrasts between a progressive Western-inspired, Westward-looking nationalism and
a revivalist, xenophobic one.

"First a revolutionary movement influenced by Western and
Japanese Meiji political doctrines developed under Sun Yat-
sen. Unlike the previous supporters of modernization, including Kang Yu-wei and Liang Ch'i ch'ao, Sun Yat-sen did not
come from the traditional literati class but rather from the new
bourgeoisie. He was, in fact, first educated in the Chinese
community of Haway, where a brother of his had settled, and
in the British colony of Hong Kong. He was trained in Western medicine and only imperfectly in the Chinese classics. In
1911 he was appointed the first president of the republic. But

the revolution was soon twisted into conservative channels, and Yuan Shi-kai's attempt at an imperial restoration followed. After that the setting up of a revolutionary nationalist regime at Canton, the May Fourth movement, and the Chinese Renaissance movement were again followed by the capturing of the nationalist leadership by Chiang Kai-shek and, after 1927, by what amounted to a gradual counterrevolution.

"From the Chinese as well as from the Japanese and Indian experiences four things seem to me to stand out clearly: (1) that contact with the West set in motion a process of change that, though there were at times stops or even switchbacks, proved, on the whole, irreversible; (2) that this was toward the acquisition of modern technology and science and toward the achievement of Western standards of living through economic development; (3) that Western political institutions were sought when they were sought as means to this end; (4) that through dialectical opposition, tradition and modernization influenced and penetrated each other so that certain traditional values could be incorporated into the process of modernization, but that the general trend has been toward more and more modernization.

"This is, I think, self-evident in the case of Japan; it can be shown also in the case of China. It is not clear at all in the case of India. But this is because India, unlike China and Japan, was a colony. If Indian nationalism developed primarily as a political movement, it was because about the turn of the century the Indian elite began to realize that the severance of the colonial relationship was the pre-condition for economic development and a total process of modernization.

"The colonial relationship is marked by a basic, inner contradiction. By bringing Western, modern civilization into contact with backward or stagnant societies, it starts the process of modernization; but it is bound to set a limit to that same process the moment it threatens the economic exploitation and political rule of the colonial power. Colonialism substitutes a commercialized capitalist economy for a subsistence, agricultural, self-sufficient one, but it prevents accumulation of capital by taking most of the surplus out of the country; it provokes a demand for goods, it creates a market, but it prevents the development of an industry for the production of those goods, and so forth. In a word, colonialism creates certain conditions for economic development and then it thwarts and distorts that same economic development to make it suit the needs of the economy of the colonializing country. All this explains why the process of modernization is usually associated in the colonial countries with the development of a strong nationalist movement. But political goals and political institutions are largely looked upon as instrumental. The adoption of democratic forms of government by the ruling elites in most countries emerging from the dissolution of colonialism should not deceive us. They were inherited from the last stage of colonial rule. They were associated in the mind of the ruled with high standards of living, scientific and technological progress, economic development, and the military strength of the former rulers and were therefore given the benefit of a trial. But in Asia, wherever the process started, democracy is already on the defensive or it has failed. It has become new, basic, guided or whatever else, or it has given way to plain military or civil dictatorship. Free institutions, I repeat, are not looked upon as an essential component of modern society, as the very foundation of its stability, but as a means toward other ends.

"Communism is just another of such means. It has been pointed out here that nationalism is not the same thing in the developing as in the developed countries. Nor is communism. To us Westerners, the antinomy of communism versus liberal

democracy is primary and irreconcilable. When I say us Westerners I mean both liberals and communists. To the Western
liberal the transition from a capitalist liberal democracy to a
socialist communist state is a lapse, is a step backward, for it
implies the destruction of a patrimony of values which he
thinks are an essential part of the modern world and were
achieved as a result of the liberal revolution. To the Western
communist who knows his Marx, the establishment of a socialist society is the result of the inner contradictions which mark
the full development of capitalism and is therefore a step
forward in historical development.

"To the Asian or to the African neither of these concepts has
much meaning. On the one hand, there is no set of values
inherited from the liberal revolution to be preserved in his
conception of the modern world; on the other hand, to him the
establishment of a socialist communist society cannot be the
'next stage' in the development from a capitalist society which
does not exist or in any case is far from having reached the
maturity foreseen by Marx. So in the developing countries
communism is *not* the antithesis of capitalist liberal democracy; it is *an alternative* to it, equally acceptable on a purely
pragmatic basis, as a way, or as a short cut, to national independence, agrarian reform, economic development, the spread
of education, scientific and technological progress, industrialization, and so forth.

Lack of understanding of this character of an alternative
that communism has in the emergent countries accounts, in my
opinion, for some failures of American policy in Asia. Take, for
instance, neutralism or noninvolvement. It simply could not enter into Mr. Foster Dulles' puritanical mind that those people
could be neutral or remain noninvolved in the struggle between good and evil, between truth and error, or that they
should be so stupid as to refuse to be helped in achieving

salvation. And of course from his point of view he was right. The trouble is that he was looking at things from *his* point of view.

"This conception of communism is derived from the prophets of the New Dispensation rather than from those of the old. I doubt that Mao Tse-tung and even Ho Chi-minh, who is the most Westernized among Asian communist leaders, ever read Marx or Engels. They certainly *have* read and meditated upon Lenin and Stalin. The classic of Asian communism is not *Das Kapital;* it is Lenin's *Imperialism as the Last Stage of Capitalism.* This offers a way out of a contradiction that has always greatly embarrassed the pro-Western intelligentsia in the colonial countries. Western civilization, which the Westernizers upheld as the source of all enlightenment, was also the source of the degradation of their own country. How could they reconcile the lofty ideals of liberalism and democracy with the reality of colonial domination and exploitation, or Stuart Mill, Burke, and Paine with the Colonel Blimps of the Indian Army? Lenin, by making capitalism alone responsible for imperialism and colonialism, provided a communist alternative to Westernization free of the burden of historical guilt that goes with colonialism.

"Moreover, Lenin with his *Imperialism as the Last Stage of Capitalism* and Stalin with his writings on *Nationalism and the Colonial Question* had reached, some thirty or forty years in advance, that same conclusion that we reached last week around this table: that nationalism is a different thing in the developing and in the developed countries. Marx and Engels had dismissed nationalism as a result of capitalist contradictions and a device by which the capitalists tried to distract the workers from the class struggle. Lenin and Stalin held that *so it was* in capitalist countries, but *not* in the colonial or semicolonial countries. Capitalism having become a world-wide phenomenon, Lenin argued, revolution, too, must be conceived in global terms: the nationalist movements in colonial and semi-colonial countries, directed as they were at the overthrowing of the capitalist yoke, became objectively a factor of the world socialist revolution even if bourgeois in character. In those countries, Stalin said, the proletariat must therefore join in an anti-imperialistic, nationalist front with the national bourgeoisie, the peasants, and the intellectuals, and convey the tremendous amount of energy thus released in the direction of the world proletarian revolution.

"This doctrine, further developed by Mao Tse-tung in his conception of a *New Democracy,* made communism a leading force in the struggle for independence in most colonial and semicolonial countries.

"But communism does not cease to appeal to the ruling elites in the emergent countries even after the struggle for independence is over. Basing our thinking on our own experiences, we are inclined to think of the political revolution as at the concluding stage of the revolutionary process. In the colonial countries, as we have seen, the opposite is true. The political revolution, that is, the achievement of independence, is but the precondition for economic and social transformation. Once independence is achieved, the ruling elites find themselves confronted with a desperate task: they have to turn a dependent, distorted economy into an independent and viable one, and they must develop this economy at a rate sufficiently quick to meet the fast growth of a population which is already living on the border of starvation. It is only natural that they should be tempted to do it the Stalinist way. It entails a ruthless cutting down of consumption and therefore suffering, starvation and death; but this fate their countries would meet all the same if they did not develop quickly enough. And as we have noted already, to develop you need capital investment; capital investment requires saving, and how can saving be obtained except by compulsion from a population which has hardly enough to live upon? What gives communism its chance in the emergent countries is that rightly or wrongly it appears to the ruling elites—not to the proletariat that does not exist—as a way, sometimes as the only way, to development and as a short cut to modernization.

"Perhaps there is something to be said in favor of this interpretation of communism. There is already some historical evidence supporting it. Marx prophesied that communism would be established first in the most advanced capitalist countries. The opposite happened. Communism has been successful so far only in countries which remained either outside or on the fringe of the capitalist industrial liberal revolution. In such countries, even though it has failed in its ultimate aims and the egalitarian stateless myth is likely to remain a myth forever, it has fulfilled historical tasks that in the capitalist countries had been accomplished by the bourgeois revolution: national unity and independence, an agrarian transformation freeing the peasants from oppressive landlordism and from a feudallike network of relationships, the accumulation of capital, capital investment, and industrialization. This does not mean for a moment that communism in those countries is more liberal. Of course it is not. But it provided a powerful vehicle of modernization where other alternatives failed.

"The case of China is typical. All the attempts to modernize the country made by the more enlightened Confucian scholars, by the Kang Yu-wei reformist movement, by Sun Yat-sen's revolution, by the May Fourth and Renaissance movements, and by the Canton Kuomintang were frustrated by the resistance or reaction of the conservative forces. All the potential usurpers in turn showed that they did not possess enough modernizing virtue and this was what made the mandate of heaven eventually fall on Mao Tse-tung. The founders of the Communist Party, men like Ch'n Tu-hsiu or Li Ta-ch'ao, were intellectuals with an antitraditional background who had been followers of Dewey's liberalism and had supported the democratic movement until they hoped this would be able to modernize China, but who switched over to communism when they felt that a communist revolution was the only way to effect a breakthrough. When the October Revolution broke out in Russia, Li Ta-ch'ao, one of the Communist Party founders, hailed it in a famous article published by the review *Youth* as 'the ever young spirit of the world, shaking from itself the dust accumulated by centuries.' This is what communism was to the Chinese and is today to most of the emergent peoples. As to freedom, it does not, I am afraid, come into this picture as an essential component. At least freedom as institutionalized in the West. I hate the fact, but I am not too pessimistic about it. As I said earlier in our discussions, society takes care of itself by ways which are often devious, and freedom is bound sooner or later to assert itself again. What is happening in the USSR and in other eastern European countries gives some reason for hope. In what forms it will do so I do not know, nor do I venture to predict. It is not the historian's business to make predictions or to construct theories. His business, like that of the field worker, is to provide some of the relevant facts out of which political decisions are made or theories constructed. Time is a dimension of the human world and the historian's area is the past. After all, this distinction between past and present is largely artificial, for the past flows into the present, and the present is but a concretion of the past."

Borsa's statement afforded Reissman a golden opportunity to highlight the profound difference between a historical and a sociological attitude. There was no general discussion after Borsa concluded but rather a single extended comment by

Reissman. Even though the debate did not continue because
time was up, there was also the general feeling after the two
had finished that little remained to be said for the moment.
Reissman's comments below will be paraphrased, but they are
close to the original statement.

Borsa's presentation, said Reissman, made it clear that India,
Japan, and China experienced a historical development similar
in major particulars to that of the West. It is evident, indeed,
that the main outlines of Westernization have been followed
by many countries. Westernization, understood in its broad
sense, is therefore not a single, unique, historical experience
but rather a general, repetitive series of social events. "However, I missed a clear element of dynamics in Borsa's presentation. He preferred to place events in a metaphysical historical
sphere—that these things happened through their own internal
dynamics."

In both the West and in today's emergent countries the
process of development is pushed and more or less directed by
the emerging elites: the bourgeoisie in the West, the nationalistic new middle-class elites in the other developing areas of
the world. In transitional periods, when those elites are trans-
forming society in order to assure their own continuation in
power, they themselves guide the process of national development as much as possible. When the process is not one of
deliberate guidance—and it need not be—it is still possible to
explain change in such societies in terms of what that elite
wants and what it is willing to relinquish in order to gain it.
Hence the English bourgeoisie promulgated liberalism in the
nineteenth century in order to gain ascendancy over the
landed aristocracy and the nobility. They had no thought of
extending the benefits of liberal democracy to the mass of
English peasants and urban proletariat, as is evident in their
own writings and actions. Only through the continued pressure

exerted by these disenfranchized groups were the benefits of liberal democracy widened to include ever more segments of society.

The same process is certainly evident today in the developing countries, as well as in those others which have not yet become truly national communities. Generally the steps seem as follows: Western technology and economic assistance are the first elements accepted, for through them the nationalizing elites hope to raise their standards of living and thereby ensure their own continuing dominance. The acceptance of these features of the modernizing process necessarily carries with it certain consequences, many of which are either unforeseen or deemed to be unimportant to the final goal. Urbanization, for example, is one such development that follows ineluctably from technological growth and industrialization. Persons migrate to the city and with that change undergo a complex series of other social changes and readjustments as a result—in family forms, religious practices, personal interaction, motivations, aspirations, etc.

As long as the elite can maintain their position, they see no need and have no desire to adjust to these further elements of the nationalizing process. Specifically, they have no desire to democratize the political structure or to tamper any further with the class structure. In the context of this analysis, for example, land reform can be seen as a mere political expedient to keep the bulk of the peasantry more or less content, but above all to make them identify with the new order and with the ends of the new elite. However, it becomes increasingly difficult for the new elite to maintain their position with impunity. Industrialization can run afoul; agricultural practices may not contribute to a higher economic standard; urban centers become cluttered with the unemployed and slum housing, and various dissatisfactions give rise to competing political ele-

ments which threaten the elite. The result is that some conces-
sion must be made by the leadership groups if they are to
continue in power.

Reissman continued, "If the Western experience is the standard—and I believe we have pretty much agreed that it is—
then the transitional process requires finally that the elite more
directly involve the population in the nationalizing process. In
short, they must extend more political liberties, they must create political institutions that seem to satisfy the greatest number—at least to give them a regularized means of voicing and
settling their complaints and of finding satisfaction within a
structured and accepted framework of action." Furthermore, it
must become evident to the elite that therein lies their own
salvation and their own long-run success. By making opportunities regularly available to a wide spectrum of the population,
the success of the nation as a whole is more likely to be assured. Hence the class structure should become more open and
more based on achievement than before. Indeed, this was the
plea of the nationalizing elite from the beginning, but they have
always wanted to stop the process once they themselves have
achieved their own success. Now it becomes clear that the
process cannot be stopped if the goal of a complete nation-
state is to be achieved. "As more and more individuals in the
society come to achieve under the 'new' order, then they become more and more committed to a continuation of the new
social and political structure, thus in turn adding further support and stability. They become integrated into society in this
real sense, rather than remaining outside of it as they had been
when a peasantry condemned to the same position for life.
Society, in its turn, also gains from this openness, because it is
then able to benefit from the best talents that it comprises. In
this sense the argument of the classical economists is quite

correct—but only if the system continues to be open to all."

The instability of societies in transition in Latin America, the Middle East, and India, for example—is obvious. Such instability is at least partially the result of elitist attempts to stop the process of nationalization in midstream, so to speak. The middle-class groups, having achieved their position, have no desire to continue the process, especially when they are convinced there is no need to give up more of their power and prerogatives. Of course they do not act so consciously, but because of their more or less incorrect interpretation of their situation. For example, even a dictator can be accepted by such groups as a short-run means of staying in power without surrendering too much to the other, larger segments of the population.

Nationalism, however, cannot succeed unless the major groups in the population are committed to that ideology—and committed to it as a viable way of life for themselves as well as others. This means that all social sectors come to accept a national political arrangement, with its requisite institutions, as a fair and equitable public style, in much the same way as an earlier feudalism was accepted as the most equitable system possible. By shaking that centuries-long tradition in the first place, however, the nationalizing elites pretty much destroyed tradition as a basis for social solidarity. "By questioning the validity of those traditions for their own purposes to begin with, they opened the door to continued questioning of their own acts. And it is through that open door that the vast bulk of the population begins to agitate for its demands and for its rights." Education, urbanization (with its increased social contacts, communications, and participation), and industrialization (with its increased possibilities for a higher standard of living)—all of these contribute to the forces that finally push a society toward full nationalism. "Anything short of that is stagnation, revolt, or fruitless attempts to return to things as they were."

Mr. Reissman concluded, "What I have tried to show is that Borsa's historical description is supported by real social and political forces at work. It is not accident or a historical metaphysics at work. It is not, as he suggested, that once a new nation buys part of the Western package—say, technology—that it must also buy with it Western reason and Western political institutions, simply because they are all glued together. They are not so glued together in any metaphysical sense. Rather, the new elites are forced into accepting all the other features of the 'package' they buy for the same dynamic reasons that the Western elites had to buy them earlier. It is in this sense, then, that the Western experience of a nationalizing history was a 'necessary' development. For the same reasons, too, it is 'necessary' for the developing nations as well if they are to achieve successful political and social integration of the nation and continuing development."

This exchange was one of the major integrating moments of the entire conference. It also came at a fitting time. Apter had introduced projections into the future. Gallagher had summed up the meeting itself. Borsa had given us historical distillation as a help toward predicting the course of events in Asia. And Reissman attempted a wrap-up, relating European to non-European experience, case studies to dynamic social theory, and specifically the theme of nationalism to the broader question of total development.

These survey and summary sessions came about three-quarters of the way through the sessions, permitting time for retrospectives and prospectives before adjournment.

III. POLICIES OF NATIONAL INTEGRATION IN THE WORLD CONTEXT

During the last century it was taken for granted that nationalism was a steppingstone to internationalism. Now one of the most common laments about the developing countries is that they are becoming nationalistic at the very moment that "political logic" calls for regional organization. These hoary arguments were not repeated in their classical form during the discussion of the international aspects of political development. By assuming a particular set of relations beween the individual and the state as a portion of the definition of nationalism, we also presumed that multicultural units can be nations. Thus, when Borsa spoke of a growing European unity, he commented that "a new European state might well be a new *national* state." The debate, then, took the form of discussion concerning the relationship between existing political divisions and institutions and the desirable *physical* description of national organization.

Mazrui, for example, strongly favored political integration of the newly independent African states. He saw hope for his aspirations in the weakness of the new governments and in their lack of tradition. The task of integration should be easier when there is no already established state; regional unification should not be as difficult for Tanganyika as for France. "There is less plural objection to major decisions in a country which has just emerged into independence under few but enormously powerful leaders. But it may also be that a leader, in guiding his country into wider federation, is in fact exercising his last act of leadership."

Apter countered with the argument that what is in fact emerging in Africa is a series of intermediate links and associations which are meaningful, functional, and can possibly lead to stronger ties. Among these tentative moves are "a kind of pan-Africanism of some political parties; international trade union meetings coupled with an effort to establish all-African organizations of many different kinds; pseudo-diplomatic proceedings and pseudo-voluntary organizations. It is sometimes misleading to consider only the legal aspects of supranational relationships in Africa."

Bayne in turn disputed Apter's construction. He argued that in Africa the internal political issue is all-important and that supranational ties are designed primarily to strengthen individual national units. "If Nyerere helps the Angolan rebels, it is to help them build their own national state." For any existing government, he concluded, sovereignty is of far more interest than regionalism of any kind, as can clearly be seen in the Ethiopia-Somali dispute over grazing lands. There the principal issue on both sides is sovereignty—overriding all other considerations of economic rationality, pan-Africanism, anti-imperialism, and so on.

Radway, too, entered the discussion, bolstering Bayne's point. "Functional associations may in fact carry you a certain distance," he said, "but beyond a given point a country may well run into a primary political requirement of development —mobilization of its populace. Conflict with neighboring states may well serve this function. Perhaps we can thus explain at least in part the persistence of separatism."

Reissman and Ibish also cast their votes against the possibility, in the case of the former, and the desirability, in the case of the latter, of attempting truly strong and functional supranational organization without the pre-existing nation-state. Reissman said that "The forces needed to create a nation and establish cultural sovereignty militate against supranational identifications or the building of supranational unities." Ibish spoke against the "monstrosity of the idea of world citizenship" and the constant "dwarfing" of the individual by the growth of ever bigger and more impersonal and less culturally defined collectivities.

This exchange was prompted by Mr. Eayrs, chairman of this session on international politics. He had opened the discussion with a written statement on policies of national integration in the present world context, in which he argued that the "state-system" is by no means disappearing. His remarks, reproduced in their entirety, follow.

"The present world context I shall interpret not as a context of art, or of science, or of religion, though these contexts certainly have their significances for national integration. My context will be the context of the political.

"I have therefore conceived my function as opening up a discussion involving two interrelated questions:

"(1) How are policies of national integration affected by the international political environment in which they necessarily take place?

"(2) What are the effects upon that environment of the policies of national integration, of the activities of the increasing number of political communities within it attempting to modernize and to develop economically?

"I will begin by commenting upon certain features of the present world context which in my view bear upon our discussion. I shall then consider their consequences both for national integration itself and for the international system.

"The *international system* I see (in an old-fashioned constitutional way) composed of three categories of political community:

"(a) All those entities calling themselves, and recognized by one another as, sovereign states (USA, USSR, about a dozen others).

"(b) Those which, though calling themselves sovereign, are

for reasons of policy denied this status by other significant members of the system (Communist China, East Germany, Vatican City, Malaysia).

"(c) Those which, not yet sovereign, are regarded by most of the remainder to be potentially admissible to the system (British Guiana, possibly Malta, conceivably Puerto Rico).

"No doubt there are a few Pago-Pago types of political community which evade this classification (where does one put Western Samoa, for example, which, though formally independent, has entrusted the conduct of its international affairs to the New Zealand government, or Bahrein?), but it will do for now.

"*Sovereignty* in this context means the right to be considered as a member of the state system: the right to claim its privileges, to meet its obligations, to participate in its peculiar rituals—it has nothing directly to do with *power*.

"The normal condition of the state-system is a condition of conflict among its members. Conflict not necessarily involving the use of armed force—though often coming to that—but rather in the sense of a continuous competition for the greatest possible share of power and influence. Sovereign states conduct their competition across a scale of antagonism. Along it governments assert themselves as best they can, employing a variety of methods. They negotiate, drawing up treaties and breaking them in the manner of the classical diplomacy. They resort to propaganda and psychological warfare. They employ economic methods of varying degrees of crudity, ranging from the subtle manipulations of central bankers to the more gross devices of boycott and embargo. They display their arms in threats of varying severity. They use their arms in varying proportions of force.

"What I have said so far could just as well characterize the very dawning of the state-system back in those days, centuries past, when Venice and Florence and Padua vied for supremacy within their restricted zones of combat. One has now to pose the more relevant question: what are the distinctive characteristics of the *modern* state-system? What distinguishes the *present* political world context of national development and national integration from that which has gone before?

"I shall deal with five of its features, two summarily, the rest more extensively.

"(1) The polarity of interstate conflict, characterized by the struggle for power and influence (between 1947 and, say, 1962) of the United States and the Soviet Union: a polarity which is, however, becoming increasingly kaleidoscopic as it is challenged by France and China, shattering, respectively, America and Soviet hegemony within the rival camps; and also as it is challenged by the governments of states, mostly in Africa and Southeast Asia, refusing to assume positions of alignment with one or the other.

"(2) The enormous concentration of wealth among a very few members of the system. More than that, the few rich are becoming richer, while the poor (as was emphasized the other day by Mr. Farmanfarmaian) are actually becoming poorer.

"Three other features of the contemporary world context seem to me to require more extended comment.

"(3) The proportions of force at the extreme end of that scale or spectrum of antagonism (of which I spoke a moment ago) have undergone, within the last two decades, an unprecedented qualitative change. The power to destroy, not just armies in the field or even civilians in cities, but whole continents and conceivably human life itself, is now at the disposal of three, possibly of four, policy makers of the state-system.

"No realistic portrayal of the problems of development—particularly one concerned, as we are concerned, with possible alternatives—can overlook one horrific alternative: a single act—considered or miscalculated as it might be—by a single representative of the entire human community could bring all development to a final and apocalyptic solution. We have heard much of the alternatives of development. Let us not forget that there is one alternative to development, and that is destruction.

"It is true that, poised like two scorpions in a jar, the great powers have so far avoided destruction. But their peace, if one can call it that, is a precarious peace, a deterrence too delicate for comfort. Technical malfunction, individual derangement, political miscalculation, each in its own way poses the continuing risk of annihilation by accident.

"(4) A fourth feature of the present political world context follows. Within the international environment there is less and less correlation between power and influence. The traditionally powerful no longer wield the influence to which their power would, in former days, entitle them; those with little power are acquiring influence out of all proportion to such power as they possess. The great powers—reckoned great on the conventional indices—are paralyzed by power. They possess an excess capacity to destroy. They are, in a sense, the first victims of the age of overkill. They are, as Stanley Hoffmann has said, like the albatross in a poem by Baudelaire, whose wings were too heavy to allow it to take to the air.

"The albatross waddles helplessly on the shore, while all about aerobatic birds of prey dip and wheel with abandon, stealing food from his beak. So Mossadegh got his refinery, Nasser his canal; so Chiari of Panama (or his successors) will get their canal.

"Lacking the means to manipulate their domestic environment, the leaders of newly independent and/or economically retarded societies are able and encouraged to manipulate the international environment. They cannot (usually) tell the great powers what to do; but they make it difficult, if not impossible, for them to do what they might otherwise want to do. Small powers have acquired the role of interpositors in international affairs.

"(5) I comment, fifthly and finally, on the tendency of new entrants to the state-system to suppose themselves immune, at least in their relations with each other, to its pitiless laws. Here I generalize from very different kinds of relationships: those of the two countries of North America; of the countries of the interwar and immediately postwar commonwealth with their vaunted *inter-se* doctrine; the countries calling themselves peoples' democracies composing a socialist commonwealth; the countries calling themselves Islamic republics composing (according to at least one Pakistani political scientist) a Muslim commonwealth; the countries sending delegations to Africa's unity congresses. All these, it seems to me, have this much in common: all of them, at one time or another, suppose themselves, by virtue of their common tradition and background, to be outside and above the state-system and free—even obliged —to devise their own rules, their own rituals, their own principles of conduct. In relation to these principles, those of the established state-system are demonstrably less efficient and assuredly ethnically inferior: less efficient because more likely to lead to war; ethically inferior because of the free play they allow double standards of morality, *raison d'état* and the kind of sharp diplomatic practices known to the Italian city-states as *combinazione*.

"The earliest, the primary, policy response of governments guiding their peoples into the state-system for the first time is *isolationism*. You keep your principles by keeping your distance. So American presidents from Washington to Harding vowed to keep their country free from the entangling alliances of the European system. So India kept out of, and scorned those Asian powers who entered, regional security organizations formed on Western initiatives.

"But isolationism does not long remain a satisfying stance for new states, just as it is not enough to remain merely immune to the harsh imperatives of *Realpolitik*. They can hope, they *do* hope, for more than mere immunity. For if in their fraternal relations one with another their example glows brightly through the encircling gloom of the international anarchy, they may move others to follow their example. They have a civilizing mission.* The neutrality of isolationism gives way, sooner perhaps than their resources objectively permit, to a neutrality of commitment—to 'positive neutralism' as it is pridefully known to its practitioners. And the number of governments practicing, or proposing to practice positive neutralism, coincides almost exactly with the number of states joining the state-system during the last five or ten years.

"So much for these personal views of the present political world context, the international environment in which national integration and national development occur.

"What are the consequences of this environment for national integration and national development?

"I'll put five of these before you, as I see them. (That there are others I don't doubt for a moment.)

"(1) One is that the alternatives for development—political, social, and economic—have been articulated and sharpened more than would otherwise have been the case as a consequence of the struggle for power and influence between the protagonists of what is called the Cold War.

"(a) In the earliest and crudest manifestations of this struggle—in the form in which it was waged by the Voice of America and expressed by such Western spokesmen as Foster Dul-

---

* In Radway's terms they become more interested in goal achievement than in system maintenance.

les—the alternatives were put with little imagination and less insight as 'the Western way of life' on the one hand and godless communist imperialism on the other. Or, if it were Mr. Gromyko who was speaking, it would be the struggle between the camp of socialist proletarian democracy versus exploitative capitalist imperialism. This debate, as I think Professor Borsa emphasized yesterday, did not mean very much to those toward whom it was directed.

"(b) Accordingly, somewhat later on the alternatives were represented by a struggle between two types of democracy: the Westminster or congressional model, on the one hand, and the one-party system, on the other. Even as recently as a couple of years ago these alternatives still regularly appeared in the propaganda of the two camps. Today, when the two-party system is more accurately seen as an amiable anachronism rather than a model of development, these alternatives are passé. Cf. Abu's cartoon: Afro-Asian prime ministers outside Westminster. One says to the other: Don't be too discouraged; of course it takes time to adapt the one-party system to these alien surroundings.

"(c) The antithesis of the Indian low-coercion system of development and modernization, proceeding essentially by the techniques of friendly persuasion, versus the Chinese high-coercion system, proceeding by its techniques of washing brains or blowing them out. This, I believe we agreed last week, is the crucial confrontation. To what degree of totalitarian control must expectant peoples subject themselves, or be subjected to, if they are to achieve the conditions for a modernized and developed society?

"(2) A second consequence of the present world context for national development consists in the tremendous exertions made by the protagonists in the Cold War to convert to their respective camps expectant peoples through contributions to their economic well-being. Western governments and white peoples have been prepared to 'blow the dough' on foreign aid; and though a reaction may be setting in among United States congressmen, it is a reaction which cut back foreign aid from $4 billion to $3.5 billion in fiscal year 1964—still a sizable and significant commitment.

"Without the struggle for supremacy between the United States and the USSR, the modernization and development of expectant peoples would have fallen far short of what they are today, inadequate as they still may be.

"History is hard enough without indulging in hypothetical history, but let me advance this hypothesis for your consideration: without the Cold War, expectant peoples would not yet have been roused to their existing posture of expectancy. Expectant people are thus the beneficiaries of the Cold War: one could even argue that it is to their advantage to keep its protagonists at odds rather than to bring them together. I will not argue that, but I will argue that it is arguable.

"(3) The sovereign state-system, assuming as it does the fictional equality of all members, notwithstanding enormous disparities of power, has made the sovereign state immensely attractive as the instrument or vehicle of development. The acquisition of statehood, the exploitation of its prerogatives, become in themselves status symbols of modernity. Even more than national air lines or steel mills, the mechanisms of the modern state offer the elites of developing societies alluring and in the main irresistible opportunities to catch up with and surpass the elites of the established state-system. The stars of the diplomatic firmament of the last five or ten years have been, more often than not, Afro-Asian rather than Western. True enough that their glittering performances often owe much to Western institutions and Western experiences—to Oxbridge and the Ivy League, to LSE and MIT, Aberdeen and

Lincoln, Camberley and Leavenworth, Rhodes Scholarships and scholarships to the Moscow University of Workers and Toilers. But for all that the state-system serves non-Western society very well as a springboard to modernity. It helps charismatic leaders hold on to their charisma. Without it, a Tito (or a Castro or a Sukarno) would not be so firmly seated in his respective saddle.

"(4) Whether—and here I come to my fourth consequence —all this fosters or hinders national integration depends on the nature of the political community in question.

"Where the political community is a nation-state, in the classical (possibly non-Silvertian) sense of a coincidence of the cultural and ethnic inheritance with political frontiers, that political community has conferred upon it by the present world context great incentives for stability, cohesion, modernization—nationalism (in the Silvertian sense).

"But where the political community presents the characteristics of communalism—where you have tension between two or more national groupings within the confines of a single state—the world political context is likely to intensify internal disarray. A minority regarding itself as the victim of majority rule will want itself to become a majority. Secession from the existing political community is an easier way of becoming majoritarian than killing off a more powerful opposition.

"Here there is an attractive alternative of political development: secession, *viz.* partition. Partition is rarely a peaceful solution. It involved the killing of thousands in Ireland, of millions in India. It is in a sense no solution at all, signifying as it does the final failure of reconciliation systems to reconcile, of legitimation systems to legitimate. But we shall see, I think, more of partition as time goes by, not less. We may see it in India, in a cruel undoing of Nehru's nation-building after Nehru goes. We may see it (as Mr. Des Alwi has hinted) in

Indonesia. We may see it in the Sudan. We may see it in Canada, where a sizable proportion of the French-speaking elite, dissatisfied with its terms of partnership with the English-speaking, prefers to go it alone, as an independent sovereign state of Quebec, rather than put up any longer with the indignities of English majoritarian rule. The opponents of separatism scoff at these pretensions: an independent Quebec, they say, borrowing from the economists, would not be viable. But they are wrong. Viability is not an economic concept. It is a political fiction. It is that condition of being looked upon by other members of the state-system *as if you were* viable. An independent Quebec, given the present configuration of this international context, would not go friendless into the world. Nor, I dare say, would an independent Bengal, or an independent African Sudan, or an independent Sumatra.

"(5) A fifth consequence for political development derives from the existence within the state-system of those terrifying weapons systems based on nuclear bombs and ballistic missiles. I've left this aspect of the subject to the last because I find it deeply perplexing. I offer only a couple of tentative comments.

"One is that the decision to acquire nuclear weapons, to become an atomic power in a military sense, may be regarded, perhaps should be regarded, as a form of political alternative rather than a straightforward policy decision. It is a policy decision, to be sure, but one so freighted down with political and moral significance as to transform in a qualitative sense the political community daring to step over that threshold dividing nuclear powers from the rest of the world.

"At first glance it would seem that the existence of nuclear weapons reinforces that missionary zeal of new nations of which I spoke a moment ago, giving urgency and content to their political messianism, even adding substance to their claim to ethical superiority. But this on their part may be making only a virtue of necessity. No government, it seems to me, requiring nuclear weapons for defense and able one way or another to acquire them will maintain for very long a position of atomic abnegation. It will be instructive to follow closely Indian atomic energy policy during the months after the inevitable Chinese detonation.

"Charles Gallagher spoke yesterday of our neglect of the individual in our discussions, and I had thought of trying to remedy this deficiency. I had, for example, thought of suggesting that to the facts of nuclear life and death people out of the line of fire—out of the line, one might better say, of first and retaliatory strikes—seem largely indifferent. I had thought of suggesting that people in the line of fire react in different ways: some marching on Aldermaston, others cultivating their gardens. I had thought of stating that the general effect upon the nuclear family (if I may borrow that term from the sociologists to describe the human condition in the atomic era) has been to make its members respond to the events of their time and place more brutally, more cynically, than might otherwise have been the case. So that a blunting of sensitivity, a slighting of values, a corroding of the civic culture, is evident all across the board. But then, of course, I realized that this line of speculation could not possibly satisfy behavioral scientists, so I abandoned it abruptly.

"I conclude with three brief observations concerning the other side of the story: the effects of national development upon the world political context.

"(1) Membership in the state-system will continue to increase, ideologies of African unity and Arab unity and Communist unity and North Atlantic unity notwithstanding.

"The sovereign state, which appeared and still appears to

many Western intellectuals to have outlasted its influence and usefulness, is more than ever here to stay. In the early 1950s, when the United Nations acquired its present site on the East River from the ever-giving Rockefellers, the architects concerned wisely sought political advice respecting the amount of accommodation they ought to provide. They were told that the maximum number of delegations by 1970 would be 106. In 1964 there are already 113, with perhaps twenty others still to come. In the files back home into which I stuff newspaper clippings the first file is Aden. The last is Zanzibar. Yemen comes before Zanzibar. World government comes before Yemen. There is more in my Yemen file than in my world government file

"(2) This suggests, as a corollary really, a second effect upon the state-system of national development and integration: the system will remain largely unaffected by appeals to supranationalization. I can see no evidence which I find impressive to indicate that what Mr. Mazrui suggested yesterday might be taking place is actually taking place: that the drive toward integration does not stop short at existing political frontiers but transcends these, spilling out and over into functional regional institutions larger than sovereign state size. I know he will remind me of the East African Common Services Organization. Charles Gallagher yesterday, in advancing what I jotted down as 'Gallagherian Theory of Galactism,' reminded us of the European Common Market and the Comecon. But what is impressive about these institutions is not the extent to which they have sublimated or taken over the roles of the sovereign states, but precisely the extent to which the sovereign states, despite the hopes of the founding fathers of supranationalism, cling tenaciously to their prerogatives and remain firmly in control of policy. And do so with the apparent support of dominant elites and of most of their followers.

"(3) This is not to say—and this is my closing observation —that in the world political context there will not develop new institutions, new procedures, to cope with the instabilities and collisions of the members of the state-system. On the political side, for example, one can foresee, one can perhaps already see, a more effective capacity, exercised through the United Nations, for dealing with the sort of brush-fire warfare now going on in Cyprus or Malaysia than the improvisation of emergency forces for Egypt in 1956 and the Congo in 1960. Similarly, on the economic side one can see at work new institutions for channeling foreign aid, extending technical assistance, minimizing instability in commodity prices, and, in general, trying to bridge the gap between the rich nations and the poor. But I must insist that these efforts are made within the context of the state-system, by sovereign states for sovereign states. So it will continue, not necessarily for all time, but for as long as a student of politics, as distinct from a political scientist, has any business looking ahead.

"And that, *chers collègues,* is as far as I can, or care, to take the subject on my own. I call now upon the area specializers, conceptual frameworkers, simple empiricists, and even upon that faceless, nameless category that Alan Horton yesterday described as 'others,' to carry the discussion forward, whether on the terms I've presented it or on any others you care to devise."

Mr. Eayrs' realistic analysis primed the discussion of nationalism versus supranationalism we have already mentioned. Another significant exchange revolved about the distinction between power and influence and the difficulties the advanced nations seem to be having in working their will on the less developed. Eayrs sustained the point that aspiring nations have to have some basic resources before they can be recognized as states, but that after that point power becomes an entirely relative and in a way insignificant matter. "As Churchill said of Malta, you don't give a constitution to a battleship. But thereafter, recognition of a government as a member of the state-system is in itself viability."

Silvert argued, however, that absolute as well as relative power must always be taken into account in judging how successful any particular policy may be. Very often, for example, the United States cannot force such materially weak and small societies as Cuba or Vietnam to follow its lead because American leadership is not sure of what it wants, or what it desires may be impossible of attainment, or the policy may demand such enormous amounts of power for its application as to make the possible rewards shrink in significance. Power, then, must be assessed in its "kinetic" or potential form as well as in its actual application, and objectively as well as relatively. Brazil, to take a recent case, exercised its power in denying certain economic measures deemed desirable by the United States for the containment of inflation. In many other fashions, too, Brazil, until the deposition of President Goulart in 1964, was creating power, so to speak, by attempting an "independent" foreign policy in the hemisphere. Whether "good" or "bad" policy, these Brazilian moves gave that country an international significance it had not previously had. Many other lands remain nonentities of the international scene because they have not passed the threshold of becoming a threat, of acquiring an international meaning.

Eayrs then asked Silvert whether he could "imagine an interactive process between international and national identity, where the fact of acquiring international meaning would have a bearing upon the national integration process?" This question picked up an earlier theme. Eayrs had stated that many leaders of developing countries were "good on the road," that they picked up prestige at home by earning it abroad. Silvert, in riposte, had stated that sometimes the reverse was true. What may be "good" internationally may sometimes be the opposite of what is "good" at home. He cited many Latin American cases—to the vigorous head-nodding of Gómez Millas —in which success at inter-American meetings could well be political suicide in domestic affairs. Eayrs, by his question, wanted Silvert to specify to what extent power is generated entirely through internal political arrangements or supplemented by international affairs.

Silvert pleaded that he was not equipped to come up with any general rules, but that certainly in the case of Argentina an interaction between domestic and international politics was evident. The progressive breakdown of Argentine government since 1930 has certainly dampened that country's ambitions in Latin America and has removed it from its earlier imperialist pretensions in South America. In addition, internal weakness has not only opened the door to international maneuverings but has also induced some Argentine governments to seek assistance from abroad for entirely domestic political purposes. The government of Arturo Frondizi (1958–1962), for example, successfully used American support for a time in keeping certain political—and especially military—opponents at bay.

The point of all this discussion, according to Silvert, is that the pattern of international politics is set in its broad outlines by the nature of the polities involved. The relationships between nation-states are qualitatively different from those pertaining between a nation-state, say, and a prenational society. In this view supranational organization is primarily a structure of only delegated powers, resting upon no autonomous authority because such institutions do not stand rooted in any particular human community.

Gallagher supported this view and capped the session by discussing the peculiar case of pan-Arabism. Here we find that the myth of supranationalism remains powerful while each country of the Arab world grows increasingly different from the others. It is true that Nasser's great international prestige (which probably transcends his purely Egyptian appeal) reinforces him at home. But it is also true that even myth thus reinforced by charisma does not serve to explain the growing effective nationalism within the Arab bloc. "The masses think of themselves as Arab," said Gallagher, "but they don't realize that they are every day more Moroccan, more Egyptian, more Iraqi."

IV. NATIONALISM, RESEARCH, AND THE FRONTIERS
   OF SIGNIFICANCE

It fell to Mr. Mazrui to chair our last full session. Because all conferences must necessarily end with the "where do we go from here" question, his agenda topic was labeled simply, "Future Research." In writing up his statement, Mazrui decided to go all the way with the questions raised about the subject in the conference outline. Thus he titled his remarks "Nationalism, Research, and the Frontiers of Significance" and discussed what is the heart of all social investigation—the determination and definition of subject.

The temperamental change which had overtaken the participants by this time may not have been consciously evident to everyone, but the minutes reveal a procedural shift which reflected a substantive one. The statements of the chairmen of later sessions were more structured than those of the first several days, but they remained spontaneous reactions to the previous discussions. And the interventions of the other participants also became much more ordered; they tended, too, to become longer and more pointed and specific and thus fewer in number. The tone of the sessions did not become deadly serious. Instead the feeling was one of harder work and less effort than in the early meetings. The humor became more subtle, the degree of mutual understanding broadened, and the comments seemed to plumb the fundamental value commitments of the discussants more and more deeply.

Some obvious as well as subtle reasons account for this change. One is that we were fortunate in having no rigid dogmatists in the group. Another is that we had grown to know each other. A third is that the move from pure theory into cases plus theory is always comforting. A fourth is that chairmen began to save up for their innings and that every one in the second week of meetings managed to add some new capital accumulated in Bellagio to the ample stocks carried to the conference. And lastly, the usual emotional lift coming with the anticipation of travel seemed to mingle with a sense of some kind of satisfaction with ourselves—fatuous as that remark may sound.

Mr. Mazrui, in his dry style and happy way with words, wrapped up the body of the discussions in the following statement.

"I am not absolutely certain what I am intended to do in this final session of discussion. The timetable said I was to talk about future research. Charles Gallagher the other day said I should fill in the gaps left by previous discussion. Someone else suggested that I should do the same sort of thing that Charles did—try to recapture some of the major moments of intellectual experience which the conference afforded. Khodadad Farmanfarmaian expressed a longing for some confessions from East Africa. I will try to do all those! Yet, first of all, would it not be presumptuous of me to recommend future research? Yes, but I will proceed to make recommendations all the same. At any rate, I will suggest some of the criteria

which are relevant in deciding whether something deserves to
be an object of research. There are at least two broad categories
of research worth doing: (a) research which produces what
we might call 'factual originality'—this is research into something which, until now, we know almost nothing about; (b) research which produces 'interpretative originality'—helping us
to look at something we do know about in an entirely different
way. ('Originality' is here used charitably.)

"Not all facts which were not known before are necessarily
worth knowing now. So here you must enter into other types
of criteria—ranging from a situation where new information
would lead to different decisions or different actions outside
the academic world to a situation where the new facts help to
cater for a curiosity let loose by some current taste. The near-
est we came to a discussion of methods of research is when
Dave Apter and Kal Silvert exchanged words as to how much
significance we should attach to what a person *says* he is—'so
cialist' or 'nationalist.' There is a level of research where what
a person says he is in a particular society tells us more about
his society if the person is a hypocrite than if he is sincere.
Supposing there I was, armed with a Rockefeller or Ford or
Carnegie grant, doing research in a brand new African society.
Someone points out to me two people—Mr. A, who is a hypocrite and says what will get him popularity, and Mr. B, who is
a sincere man. I am trying to find out whether Pan-Africanism
in this particular Central African republic is a popular ideology. I find a pamphlet written by Mr. B praising Pan-Africanism. But because Mr. B is a sincere man, all I have found
out is that Mr. B himself is a Pan-Africanist. This tells me
nothing about the popularity of Pan-African postures in this
Central African republic. But I then find a pamphlet written
by the hypocritical Mr. A—and this one is anti-Pan Africanism.
I think the hypocrite has probably given me more information
about his society than have the personal confessions of the

sincere man. The lesson to be drawn from this is that what people *call* themselves in a society may be more significant from a social point of view than what they really are.

"Another point should be noted in this matter of deciding what is 'significant.' When we discussed Professor Itagaki's paper one of the questions which pushed itself into the front was this—was Japan of interest because it was 'unique' in its path to modernization? Or was it interesting because it had features in common with other countries? Or is this a case whereby in studying what is unique about Japan you are at the same time finding out what is the general rule?

"When Kal Silvert tells a Middle Eastern specialist that what the Middle Easterner has just claimed for his area is not unique but happened in Latin America, is Kal Silvert maximizing the interest of the phenomenon? Or is he deflating its interest? Well, sometimes an African phenomenon gains a new dimension of significance when it is exposed as not being particularly unique after all. Dave Apter the other day talked about 'African socialism'—a term that means something different from 'socialism in Africa.' Nkrumah, for example, is a socialist and is, of course, an African—but he is not an 'African socialist.' But Nyerere *is* an African socialist.

"African socialism in this sense is a socialism which sees itself as a logical extension of tribal collectivism. Silvert, in *Expectant Peoples*, talks about a phenomenon of 'nationalizing socialism.' African socialism is 'socialism ethnicized' identified with the genius of peoples in the African continent. Tom Mboya, for example, discerns in African tribal life what he calls

the logic and the practice of equality, and the acceptance of communal ownership of the vital means of life—the land. [*Freedom and After*, 1963.]

"President Nyerere of Tanganyika has said that Africans did not need to be converted to socialism. It is 'rooted in our past—in the traditional society which produced us.' And partly arising out of this conviction, there is no free hold of land in Tanganyika—all is leasehold now legally. The conviction underlying all this is that African societies can proceed from tribal collectivism to industrial socialism without passing through all the stages of capitalism in the classical Western sense. And many African socialists believe that Africa is uniquely placed for such a developement.

"For me this ideological phenomenon becomes more, not less, interesting when we recall that such uniqueness was also claimed by some Russian socialists well before the Russian Revolution. In an 'Open Letter to Engels in Zurich, 1874,' a Russian socialist (Tkachoff) argued in the following vein:

Our people are permeated in the large majority . . . with the principle of communal property; they are, if I may say so, instinctively, traditionally communist. . . . From this it follows that our people, despite their ignorance, are much nearer to a socialist society than the peoples of Western Europe with their higher education.

"Engels dismissed this as a 'childish conception' emphasizing that:

Communal ownership of land . . . is an institution common to all peoples at a certain state of development.

"Engels insisted:

A bourgeoisie is . . . as necessary a precondition of the socialist revolution as the proletariat itself. A person who says that this revolution can be carried out easier in a country which has no proletariat or bourgeoisie proves by his statement that he has still to learn the ABC of socialism. [*Volksstaat* (Leipzig) 21 April 1875.]

"As for Marx himself, he just could not stand the Russian attempt to ethnicize socialism. He said as early as 1859:

A ridiculous prejudice has recently obtained currency that common

property in its primitive form is specifically a Slavonic, or even ex-
clusively Russian form. It is the primitive form that we can show to
have existed among Romans, Teutons, and Celts and even to this
day we find numerous examples, ruins though they be, in India.
[*Kritik*, 9.]

"Marx and Engels probably succeeded to an extent in reducing the interest of Russian collectivism by deflating its claims
to uniqueness. Here was a case of something being made to
appear less significant by being exposed as universal. And yet
the whole episode perhaps serves today to *heighten* the interest of similar claims to uniqueness in Africa.

"The emergence of the ideology of African socialism is a
useful example for another point I want to make. At this conference we have dwelt a good deal on modernization and its
role in creating a nation-state. More often than not we had
postulated a country with a relatively homogeneous basis of
custom like Islam. In a good many African countries today no
such homogeneous basis of custom obtains. So the process of
nation-building involves both the creation of a modern future
and the *creation* of a common past.

"David Apter in his paper talked about African nationalism
as having within it the self-image of rebirth. This is true. When
I visited the United Nations some time ago it was interesting
to listen to Nigeria's Foreign Minister as he reveled in the in-
nocence of a new nation just born. But involved in this very
concept of rebirth is a paradoxical desire—the desire to be gray-
haired and wrinkled as a nation, of wanting to have an antiquity. This is directly linked to our previous discussion on identity. In so far as nations are concerned, there is often a direct
correlation between *identity* and *age*. The desire to be old becomes part of the quest for identity. A country like Iran or
Egypt would not have a longing of precisely the kind which a
country like Kenya would have. This is where the concept of
'African socialism' epitomizes the whole paradox of African

nationalistic longings—the desire to modernize and to 'ancient-ize' at the same time. Thus the Gold Coast, on emerging into independence, first decided to wear the ancient name of Ghana —and then to modernize the country as rapidly as possible. Mali is another case of trying to create a sense of antiquity by adopt-ing an old name. In Central Africa we will shortly have a country called Malawi. And when the hold of the white minor-ity in Southern Rhodesia is broken, we will have a country called Zimbabwe. A distinguished African professor in Nigeria has been trying to get the name changed into the name of some old African state. Now, if this rechristening of countries leads to, say, teaching the history of *old* Ghana in the schools of the *new* Ghana, future generations of Ghanaians will have their sense of historical identity affected by this—even if the new Ghana does not occupy the same spot on the map as the old Ghana.

"To put it in a more specific way, there are three processes involved in an African country: (a) the erosion of tribally exclusive traditions, (b) the attempt to erect a nationally in-clusive tradition, and (c) the construction of a modern state. Sometimes the attempt to create a nationally inclusive tradi-tion merges into the process of creating a modern state. This is best illustrated in the legal sphere of the life of a common-wealth African country. Under British rule two broad catego-ries of law were operative: (a) modern, codified, usually English, principles operating in criminal and, to an extent, civil law; (b) customary African law operating in matters like marriage, divorce, and inheritance. What went under the name of 'African customary law' was, in fact, a multiplicity of laws in each country. The traditions involved were essentially of a tribally exclusive type. When I left Uganda a commission had already started the massive job of taking evidence from all groups on customary provisions on marriage, divorce, and the status of women. The object of the exercise does seem, in part, to be to distill out of these tribally exclusive traditions something which may form the basis of a new nationally inclusive common tradition. And Uganda law on these matters will then rest on that new traditional base, but bearing in mind also what will be deemed as the demands of modernization. New attitudes on marriage and divorce can, of course, let loose all kinds of consequences—ranging from the status of women to the effect this status will have on other areas of social life and even economic development.

"The selectiveness implicit in this whole idea of distilling commonality out of diverse traditions extends to other aspects of the quest for nationhood. Certainly the desire to be old and wrinkled as a nation is accompanied by a determination to have a failing memory. The secret both of national pride and of national cohesion is to know what to forget. In Kenya this secret is most acutely tested not against what happened in antiquity but against what happened during the Mau Mau insurrection. On the one hand, there is a desire that yesterday's villains—the Mau Mau fighters—should become today's heroes. On the other hand, there is a determination that yesterday's heroes—the loyalists who fought against the Mau Mau—should not become today's villains. The Mau Mau insurrection was, in a sense, a civil war—not just a civil war with the Kikuyu on one side and the rest of Kenya on the other. It was a civil war within the Kikuyu tribe itself. And yet the feat of selective recollection which we Kenyans are in the process of accomplishing has involved this question. How could we convert this tremendously divisive event in our past into a tremendously unifying heritage in our future? I don't know now —but I am sure we will convert it, as other nations before us have converted their own divisive moments in their history.

"Another theme in the conference which we might look at

again is the theme of acculturation. A good many observers talk about the impact of Western values on, say, African societies. This kind of talk becomes loose when even the desire for 'self-determination' is described as peculiarly Western. The distinction which fails to be made is between new desires and new ways of expressing old desires. If an African tribe in the early days took up arms against white intruders but based its objection to the intrusion on the ground of its being an offense to tribal ancestors, the objection was dismissed as 'nativistic' and even superstitious. But if, a couple of decades later, the same tribe objected to white intrusion on the grounds of the principle of self-determination, it is inferred that the tribe had learned to love freedom from contact with the white man. The Mau Mau insurrection turned out to be one of those borderline cases where objection to foreign domination was partly nativistic and partly Wilsonian.

"It is further assumed by some that in order to modernize, an African country must Westernize. It would still be pertinent to ask: how much Westernism is necessary for modernization? One can do away with chiefs without replacing them with, say, Western representative institutions. Mr. Kenyatta need not be converted to a lover of opera. Mr. Nyerere has translated Shakespeare's *Julius Caesar* into Swahili—but, then, the Koran was translated into English quite awhile ago without leading to an Islamization of England.

"Yet Africans cannot escape the charge of being in the process of being Westernized. If they have a multiparty system, that is Western. If they have a no-party system, that is still Western. If, like French-speaking Africans, they sometimes like to identify themselves with France, they have truly been Westernized. If, like English-speaking Africans, they are sometimes indignant against Britain, they have truly been converted to the Western value of independence. If they are God-fearing, they are products of the West. If they are atheists, they are still Westernized. If they become collectivistic, they are Western. If they are ruggedly individualistic, they are still Western. There is just no escaping this charge. It is, in fact, the latest form of Western imperialism. Of course, modernization started in the West. Let us say it started in England. How meaningful would it be to say that French society was being anglicized when it proceeded to modernize *after* England? If it would be meaningful, why don't we then continue to call this process of modernization "anglicization" if it was in England that it first *started?* Of course, this is an argument about words. But the words we use can obscure differences which should be noted. Communism is sometimes described as Western. So it is, in a sense. But your sense of 'Western' is getting weaker and weaker. It is like saying, 'Buddhism is Hinduism,' or saying, 'Christianity is Jewish.' This is true—but your sense of 'Hinduism' or 'Jewish' is getting weaker. It is weaker still when you say, 'Islam is essentially Christian,' or, 'essentially both Jewish and Christian.' Again you may have a point, but you are stretching words a bit. By the same token a modernizing process which started in the West or has Western roots will get less and less Western as it blends with non-Westernism in distant lands. And one obscures this fact when one uses a blanket term 'Westernization' to denote *any* response to the Western impact. One ought, in fact, to draw such a distinction between responding to the Western impact and actually being Westernized—Westernization itself being only one kind of response.

"The Western impact itself can in turn be categorized. Charles Gallagher raised the interesting point yesterday that it is possible to take Western technology with little Western culture—if the native culture is 'high enough.' He contrasted Japan with the Middle East, arguing that Japan felt less insecure about maintaining its own culture than the Middle East did.

"I agree with Charles that it is possible not to feel too insecure about maintaining one's culture—but I am positive it has nothing to do with high and low cultures. It seems to me there is a more obvious difference between the Arab experience and the Sino-Japanese experience than the difference of highness and lowness of culture. That is the conspicuous difference which makes colonialism a variable in assessing degrees of the Western impact—and of levels of insecurity about the survival of the native culture. This, in turn, introduces the variable of where the initiative lay in the process of acculturation.

"Far from Japan having been immune to cultural insecurity, it is arguable that her initiative in seeking the strength which comes with Western technology was partly inspired precisely by a sense of insecurity about her way of life. 'Japanese spirit, Western science' was a culturally defensive slogan. And if Japan had had direct colonial experience, the Japanese, like the Arabs, might have developed a sense of cultural insecurity *after* the harm was done—instead of in the initial stages of contact with the West when it was still possible to take the precautionary measure of industrializing in order to protect Japan's way of life.

"Let us now examine Gallagher's thesis from the angle of lowly cultures. Taking his sense of culture—to include forms of aesthetic experience—it seems to me that an educated Babuba tribesman need not feel at all insecure about the survival of, say, certain forms of drum rhythms which he has loved to listen to. These may conceivably be blended with African forms of jazz, but the sense of insecurity may be absent in the individual. And if it turns out to be there, it would not be because of the simplicity of his culture. On the contrary, we know from experience that some of the greatest pangs of cultural insecurity are felt by those whose native cultures are complex. For example, one of the reasons there is less linguistic nationalism in Africa than there is in parts of Asia is that the Asian languages concerned are often complex in themselves and in a complex relationship with the totality of the literary and religious cultures of those who speak it.

"Finally, one must compare Japan up to 1945 (when she was in a position to be selective about changes) with Japan after 1945 (when, for a brief period, she lost the initiative of her own acculturation). It is Japan after MacArthur which should be compared with the Arab world after the Anglo-French colonial impact. I would be surprised if there were no apprehensions in Japan today about 'Americanization.'

"The term 'Americanization' brings me to a somewhat different phenomenon—the phenomenon of one wing of the same culture (Europe) feeling culturally insecure about the impact of another wing (America). Here again the subcultures of Britain or France may be 'high'—but this does not prevent many Englishmen and many Frenchmen from being apprehensive about American influence. One can now even talk about Europe adopting American technology and culture—supermarkets, kitchen devices, and all. And yet Europeans can still be afraid lest the supermarket and kitchen gadgets—or even central heating—should lead to an erosion of what is best in, say, British or Italian culture. This is a case of countries feeling insecure precisely *because* they believe they have a 'high culture.'

"And yet one implicit point in Charles's thesis is of relevance. In assessing degrees of Western influence on different countries, it is not only the intensity and duration of the impact itself which should be estimated—it is also the texture of the native culture receiving the impact.

"Professor Borsa did precisely this in his paper yesterday.

But the illustration I will pick is what he mentioned later in the discussion which followed his paper. He and Professor Ibish asserted that countries with Islam as a religion have, in that religion, a shield against communism. Here is a case of looking at the texture of Islamic society and then drawing conclusions as to the degree to which it can be changed by a communist impact. And yet I am not sure that I know what is meant when I hear Islam described as pre-eminently resistant to communism. Is this the same thing as saying that he who is brought up as a Muslim cannot easily be converted to communism? If that is the assertion, then it is clearly false. At any rate, it is not self-evident to me how we can say that a Muslim is safer from conversion to Marxism than a Chinese Buddhist, Indian Hindu, or Italian Catholic. But suppose we say all these religions are, by their very texture, equally resistant to communism but not infallibly. The reason which suggests itself for the resistance is the atheistic nature of Marxism. But atheism is a form of secularism—and many of us here have postulated all along that modernization is partly defined by its increasing secularism. Isn't the logical extremity of a process of secularization the redundancy of God either as a causal hypothesis or an ethical base? Is this the direction that modernism must inevitably take? What lies beyond modernity as so far conceived? The outer frontier of research is to try to discern clues on the nature of the future from the experience of the present and the past."

Mazrui's valedictory set off an ardent discussion, as may be imagined. After all, it was also the last discussion session. Some persons just made factual comments. Ibish, for example, stated, "I just said that a Muslim has to revoke his faith in order to become a communist. He just adheres to another religion. I make no special claim for one religion's being more incompatible with Marxism than another."

Other persons tried to wrap up all their previously expressed views in the light of Mazrui's introduction. Apter argued, in this connection, that we had been skirting the moral issue, "the long-term significance of economic development in political terms—the possibility for a libertarian political ethic. Two different trends have been described here. The first is a period of discipline in which mechanisms of control must be set up in developing countries. But we have remained reluctant to say that even at this stage libertarian values have to be pushed aside, as the price to be paid for successful development. The other side of the argument may be that libertarian values will at last emerge as societies progress. This view is probably more than a merely active faith, for development is at once restrictive and liberating—it frees human reason."

Mazrui also laid bare another nagging worry: cultural integrity and the menace to it many people see in "Westernization." Whether or not the meaning of that word is blurred by its use as a synonym for "development," Mazrui's plea for a terminology which would show more essential respect for the non-European peoples did not go unchallenged, even though certainly no disrespect as such was meant for any of the emergent lands. Silvert, in talking to this point, felt called on to tell a story whose locale is an underdeveloped portion of Europe—the Eastern European *shtetl* with its village, Jewish folk culture.

The tale concerns a rather dull young man who wanted to enter the rabbinate. The local rabbi, to discourage his pretensions, told him of the intellectual demands of Talmudic reasoning. Undaunted, the youth asked that he be tested. The rabbi then posed a problem. "Two persons come down a chimney," he said, "one with his face dirty, the other with his face clean. Which one washed?" The young man answered that it was the one with the dirty face, of course. "Wrong," sadly said the rabbi. "The one with the clean face saw the dirty face of the other and so, thinking his own face was dirty, went off to wash."

The boy asked for a second chance, so the rabbi the next week asked him the same question. Forearmed, the youth answered confidently, "The one with the clean face." "Wrong," sadly said the rabbi. "When the one with the clean face went off to wash, the one with the dirty face asked him where he was going. So then, of course, the one with the dirty face went off to get cleaned up." Crestfallen, the aspiring student asked for a third and last chance.

After another week of preparation he returned to the rabbi, who repeated his question. Again with confidence the youth, now prepared to defend his point, answered that it was the one with the dirty face who washed. "Wrong," sadly said the rabbi. "Tell me, *bucher,* how can two people come down the same chimney, one should have a dirty face, and the other a clean one?"

Silvert's argument was that no two societies can come down the chimney of modernization without getting their faces similarly dirty. That does not mean that all modern societies are alike—indeed, they may develop certain enormous diversities, at least as compared with the small range of difference seen in village cultures in many parts of the world. "The fundamental question, then, is how much of and what aspects of Westernism are absolutely inescapable for a society which wants to develop? Is it possible to modernize and retain certain beliefs and practices that are absolutely incompatible with modernism? Universalistic religions, for example, inhibit relativistic determinations. They set up barriers between persons and groups, they 'particularize,' they make people in the same culture deaf to each other. In sum, then, we need first to make up our minds concerning what we see as a modern society and then ask what cultural elements may be compatible with changes toward modernism and which may not be."

Reissman supported this view by drawing on his experience as an urban sociologist. "I have been struck by the similarity," he said, "between the way we have been talking about modernization and the way in which people talked about urbanization at the turn of the century. The choices were then similar to those which face us now. If we accept this parallelism, many things in urban development simply could not be avoided, no matter how hard we tried. Westernization as a concept describes a certain repetitive character to the experience of modernization—a set of inescapable consequences of that particular kind of change."

Mazrui at this point asked Mr. Dennison I. Rusinow to comment about Yugoslavia in order to see what it is that a country at once Christian, Muslim, and Communist does about the inevitably complex hostilities which must rend it. Rusinow, who had recently become an associate of the AUFS and had driven over from Yugoslavia to attend the last few days of the meeting, gave a brief description of how individuals feel about what seems to the observer like a series of inconsistencies between that country's political aims and its many belief systems. He said that the members of the Greek Orthodox Church feel much less conflict than the Roman Catholics, who had been told that it is impossible to be both Roman Catholic and communist. Those Muslims who accept the ideal of the theocratic state are, however, the least open to suggestion from such a secular state as is that of Tito's Yugoslavia. The state, however, has so far been able to allow for this diversity of reaction, arguing that its achievements in raising living standards and in education also serve the ends of religion, even though such a result is of course not an aim of the state.

"The forms of consensus-creation in Yugoslavia are rather elementary," added Rusinow. "The government has established a balance and a counterbalance of different forces, granting advantages to keep possibly disruptive forces quiet at least for the time being. Compromise with religion, for instance, has so far been rather more on the side of the regime than of the churches. Religious leaders may well feel that they are simply going to outlive this necessary evil." As for the ancient conflict among Yugoslavia's nationalities, these have now been converted into regional economic clashes.

Rusinow's analysis prompted mention of other cases of difficult church-state relations. Bayne went into the Israel problem, remarking that there are no constitutional arrangements for settling the relationship between church and state there because the state's founders did not want to face the issue. Now, however, there may be a slow evolution toward a kind of theocracy, propelled by the new Sephardic immigrants, their orthodoxy, and their low educational estate. Mazrui returned to the argument that separation of church and state may merely establish a kind of secular religion of the political. Reissman also persisted in separating academia from social reality, asking whether what we see as a conflict between religious prescription and secularizing goals may not be sensed in that way by the human beings involved in the process. "Shouldn't one ask them how they live the conflict?" Bayne returned to freedom, religion, and development, and Rusinow pointed out that in Yugoslavia, at least, American economic assistance had blunted some of the hardship normally attendant on capital accumulation in developing countries.

Borsa had the last word. "The European industrial revolution involved a tremendous amount of coercion, even if not all of it was exerted by the state. Perhaps there is a certain amount of coercion which is just inevitable in a process of total transformation."

Mazrui then thanked the discussants and adjourned the session. It was a Thursday afternoon, with plenty of time left for packing and farewells. The group was to begin to disband the following day at noon, after a short morning session in which Silvert was to attempt an over-all assessment.

CHAPTER FOUR

A Last-Session Commentary

In his short farewell to the members of the conference, Silvert made no further attempts at a general summation. Instead he thought it would be fitting to indicate the utility of the meeting for the research planning of the American Universities Field Staff, and to sketch in how some of the interchanges were significant to the study of the comparative politics of development.

For the last four or five years the AUFS has increasingly concerned itself with comparative studies. The reasons are natural enough, given the character of the organization. All staff associates work in more than one country, and thus each inevitably engages in some comparative analysis. In addition, the organizational structure of the AUFS has fostered a resource ideally suited to comparative work: an informal community of scholars dedicated to the study of developing areas.

However, the same AUFS policies that encourage independent exploration also are impediments to joint comparative research. Associates are academically sovereign when in the field. They choose their own research subjects, employ their own methods, and within very lenient limits establish their own rhythm of work. Diversity among the associates is enhanced by the manner in which staff men are selected. The choice is not according to specific academic discipline or country of study, but rather by criteria of general competence in area studies as well as more explicitly professional identification. The AUFS emphasis on the scholar as individual and on the freedom of his working conditions is essential to its role as a risk-taker for the academic community in exploring patterns of development as well as working on the frontiers of foreign area studies.

The men who enjoy the freedom of working under the AUFS aegis pay a certain price for it in having to cope with a degree of difficulty in defining joint research subjects. They share in the common scholarly search for the most effective hypotheses and techniques for the study of development, of course. But the disciplinary diversity and the autonomy exercised by each AUFS associate require research hypotheses of a most particular level of generality if there is to be effective collaboration. Culture-bound schema must be abhorred and abjured. Sweeping generalizations describing universal functions likewise have little appeal to specialists accustomed to working finely in the intimacy of their own theaters. The problem, then, is to find research theses which will permit depth analysis of individual societies and intercultural comparison at the same time.

Such designs are not easily come by, either for the AUFS or for the field in general. The approach to nationalism and development taken in *Expectant Peoples* seems to have met our needs for comparative work, but we also were curious to know what professionals from many parts of the world would do substantively with that essay. Here you have a major reason for the interest of AUFS in this meeting. We certainly were not seeking your agreement with our particular way of handling nationalism; all we wanted to know in this regard was whether our approach transcended our own peculiar needs—whether in meeting our own requirements we also could satisfy broader academic functions. We think this gathering has demonstrated clearly enough that there is no fatal flaw in a construction of this style. Your varied opinions concerning what we have *done* with this pattern for investigating the nature of nationalism and development have been sufficiently expressed to need no recapitulation.

Naturally we also hoped that what we had to say would contribute significantly to a general theory of development, and thus we also placed much emphasis on dynamic processes and the patterns of change in themselves. As we said before, however, we probably could not expect in this meeting to flesh out in detail many of the possible combinations of institutional and value elements to be seen as societies modernize. But certainly the conference has advanced many suggestions concerning strategic cases meriting study in much greater detail.

Aside from this task of self-evaluation, AUFS had another primary selfish purpose in mind for the conference. If the nationalism and development study stood up fairly well, we wanted your assistance in suggesting approaches to what we propose as our next large-scale undertaking. The principal warning I have derived from our discussions is to be extremely alert to the implications and costs of trying to work between absolutely general theories and low-level limited generalization. The secondary *caveat* brought sharply to attention is that we must be prepared for the emotional as well as the intellectual consequences of drawing theories of development so self-consciously from a Western model as we have done. In *Expectant Peoples* we defined modern politics as being synonymous with national politics, and national politics as being correlative with a particular kind of class structure and set of social attitudes. Thus we were testing for the existence of a certain constellation of phenomena, expecting to find them only partially present in some of the societies we were studying, and almost totally absent in others. Clearly the effect of this approach must be to close out the chances of generating a theory good for all social systems, as we said during the discussions. The further effect is to provoke a special kind of controversy based on two different positions: one which holds that social theory—to be theory—should cover a broader range of human affairs; and the other that there are some areas with cultural ways of life which set them outside of such theoretical propositions as the relation we posited, for example, between social class and national orientation.

I think I may as well say baldly that we of the AUFS disagree with both these objections. The theory behind *Expectant Peoples* may not be "good," but it is not "bad" because it does not explain all political change. Perhaps its greatest weakness is that it seeks to explain positively what a modern polity is, but does not have as much strength in guiding analyses of completely nonmodern situations. As for the second argument, we persist in believing that *all* modern states must share certain characteristics—whether the point of departure toward that development is Europe, Africa, Latin America or Asia. Perhaps "color" and not class is the way Africans in recently independent countries see the heart of their present social problem, for example, but that perception of today does not mean that greater development will not raise future class problems for them. It is strange that these two arguments can sometimes be raised by the same individuals, for one pushes us into very broad generalizations and the other coaxes toward a romantic particularism which is untenable if the potential of comparative studies as a means to diagnose human behavior is to be realized.

I feel called upon to disagree with yet another opinion expressed frequently and by many of the participants. This view is that the process of social change is so complex that at least in our time little or nothing can be done to control or influence the course of the modernization process. A few persons went beyond this belief to argue that the processes were past understanding, let alone control. Whether the holders of political power in developing lands will exercise the most rational means at hand to promote modernization is obviously open to question. That there exist at least some semirational and pragmatic approaches to the techniques of development is not, however, debatable. Nor can it be argued that no states have ever had any success in attempts to promote rational and controlled development. The contemporary explosion of the social sciences, the research and developmental activities of national governments and international agencies, and the historical experiences of developing countries are creating a vast body of knowledge about social change. It must be granted that there is no single accepted body of doctrine—ideological or scientific—which can be neatly applied to the modernization problems of any country. But the fact that the question is not settled does not mean that no tentative answers at all are available, and that we must simply surrender to letting fly in order to see where the pieces will land.

One of our reasons in the AUFS for examining nationalism was the belief that we could introduce at least a bit of order into one of the most badly misused of all the words given new vitality by the political changes of the underdeveloped world. We came to this meeting with a second and analogous subject in mind—the relationship between public freedom and development. I feel we should admit that we choose themes of this kind because we hope our findings might possibly make an operational difference to policymakers as well as to other social scientists. We are not playing at Plato. We no more presume, as academic professionals, to tell political leaders what is right and proper in a moral sense than we attempt to force an orthodoxy on our own institution. But we certainly do attempt to choose research themes which we hope will have significance in helping them to make their ideological and operational choices with a fuller knowledge of the possible consequences of their decisions.

If our examination of nationalism does not succeed in indicating which elements of national identification, nationalistic ideology, and the nation-state structure promote general development, and which retard it, then the book has failed in its purpose from any point of view, whether intellectual or political.

Like nationalism, freedom is another of those terms so laden with emotion and diverse meanings as to tempt one to discard it entirely. And yet, again like nationalism, the word "freedom" is in such wide use throughout the world that to neglect an examination of its relationship to modernization should be an act of positive disavowal, not mute neglect. A further problem with nationalism and freedom as political concepts is that both are buried beneath the fat of facile judgment and propagandistic manipulation. In undertaking to study freedom and development, then, we can expect the same complaints we received concerning *Expectant Peoples*—that we should use a word other than "freedom" or, using the word, we should even forget the task of definition and employ as guide the wisdom of the stereotype. Our answer will remain the same. The assumption of objectivity, the assertion of an operational definition, and the task of data accumulation and analysis demand an effort on our part to which the reader will have to respond if he is to make a legitimate judgment concerning the validity of our premises, methods, and findings.

Let me rapidly sketch some of our present ideas concerning

how to approach the relation between freedom and development. Our treatment of the social, political, economic, and value aspects of development will gain much from this meeting. We shall also build further upon the class and nationalism postulates already advanced, adding many refinements suggested by these debates.

Prior to this conference we developed an operational definition of freedom as follows: "Freedom is the making of rational and effective public choices." Let me hastily add some detail to what may seem a simple-minded statement. When we say "making," we imply an organized, routinized, and ordered procedure for the creation of opportunities for choice as well as its expression. We refer not only to communications systems, ballot boxes, pressure groups, parties, and political arguments with friends, but also to the acceptance by whatever groups may be participant in the political process that this kind of choice-making is desirable and is to be respected.

A "rational" decision should take into account the available and relevant evidence, weighed in a pragmatic fashion. Such a decision should also maintain the possibilities of making future rational choices in as broad an area as the state of knowledge may allow. We know, of course, that many desires and value judgments will enter to impede full rationality, so that we must concern ourselves with the degree to which decisions are rationally taken and the effect of blind areas, of partial irrationality.

"Rational" decisions are in their nature "effective," for otherwise they would be irrational. A decision to take off for Mars can be rational only for someone who owns a spaceship. "Social effectiveness" as a concept has its complexities, however. Does the state, for instance, respond to the decisions implicit in an election? Does a political party grapple with the choices made by another—accepting, amending, rejecting with sense?

Is the array of choices being made so wide as to preclude compromise? If there can be no compromise, then some choices must remain wholly ineffective and coercion must be applied to groups remaining outside the consensual system.

The word "public" indicates that we propose to deal only with the social aspects of choice, not with "psychic" freedom— with the legitimate but different question of whether a man retains his innermost spark of free will even in solitary confinement and under imminent sentence of death. And finally, by "choice" we refer to a selection among two or more substantively and significantly distinct alternatives. In sum, then, this kind of freedom involves choosing among alternatives recognized as significantly different because the participants are competent to see the difference and have available to them evidence on which to base recognition and judgment. This kind of freedom assumes a social system with rational procedures that assure public consequences will flow from the exercise of choice.

We do not expect this summary description of the concept to occasion either astonishment or great conviction. We hope you will see, however, that it promises much analytical leverage when employed in conjunction with concepts of social structure and other institutional arrangements. For example, it may be useful in explaining how much reality there is in the conventional view that underdeveloped states can employ no democratic procedures because of mass illiteracy, tribalism, or the other common impediments to the formation of a national community. Let us experiment a bit, to see how we may apply our approach to this question.

If we turn away from the temptation to think of societies only in terms of averages, then it is easier to see that some groups can practice the kind of public freedom we have been talking of, while others cannot. Logical as it may seem to imagine that political unions cannot survive half free and half slave, it is clear that a lot of countries have managed the trick for long periods. Whenever there are strikingly superordinate groups in coexistence with markedly subordinate ones, the possibility exists that the former will be able to develop the styles and practices of public freedom for themselves—or, at the very least, that individuals within the group will so develop. This happening is not necessary, of course: ruling groups may develop very few of the patterns and institutions of freedom, or they may cultivate them only to discard them when the dispossessed clamor to share in their privileges, rights, and duties.

The purposes of political analysis are not served by considering the processes of nation-building only from the focus of the alienated, thus permitting the conclusion that since pragmatic, relativistic, effective decisions are denied to them, the denial extends to total societies. The job of analysis is also vacated if we presume that empowered groups are the helpless victims of their interests, that they "must" act within the captivity of their appetites. What we need to know, on the contrary, is what the values and procedures and ideas of the ruling groups are, and what kind of thralldom the dispossessed occupy. In this fashion we may approach an understanding of the dialectic between the leaders and the led and then enjoy the effort to diagnose the forms of the crises of access to the national community certain to occur among the hitherto alienated as the society feels the stresses of economic and social development.

We think, then, that the query, "Who is at least potentially free?" is worth posing for any society, and that the question has particular relevance to developing societies where economic, social, and political participation seems to be a *sine qua non* for the selfsustaining growth of the more mechanistic measures of modernization. With an answer to that question, we can then proceed to the second, which is whether those who are potentially free exercise that power, or whether they continue to be trapped in irrationality and social and political exclusionism. One of the by-products of approaching the definition of freedom in this manner is that it permits the construction of a typology of authoritarianism—a task in which political scientists have been extraordinarily lax. What we propose is the classification of nondemocratic situations according to the nature of the relations between those who exercise authority, and those who are subjected to it. An important criterion for judging the quality of this interplay is whether the leaders are able to make rational decisions within a significantly broad area, or whether they are themselves captive.

The hypothesis from which we start should by now be obvious: our research assumption is that at any given time the more widespread the practice of public freedom consistent with the competence of concerned social groups, the greater the chances that self-sustaining development will be achieved.

As a final word on this subject, it might be added that there are many ways in which partial freedom can make itself felt. In many developing countries the government holds to itself a monopoly of public decisions, but individuals exercise other freedoms: they can walk and talk freely, travel at will, read a wide range of materials, criticize openly, and so forth. Such civil liberties are in our view desirable anywhere, of course; they are a necessary part of the procedures involved in making the rational and effective public decisions of which we have been speaking. They also create the conditions for the self-adjusting nature of modern society, in which individuals fit themselves by anticipation into their social roles, thus helping to prevent breakdowns in the general social process and obviating the necessity for intimate social controls to make the complex arrangements of specialized modern life proceed. The existence of this part of the range of public freedom does not guarantee democratic participation in the policy decisions of the state, but it helps. One of our necessary chores in this research, then, will be to ask not only which groups are able to be free and actually exercise freedom, but also which freedoms they practice.

There, in very brief compass, is the thesis of our next comparative study. We shall certainly ponder the debates in this conference to find clues for this new undertaking. But the principal lesson we draw is forced on us by the relative silence on the subject of freedom and development in our discussions. Some of the disinclination to talk of the matter has seemed rooted in the conviction of some of the discussants that the question is fruitless, irrelevant either to the desires of leaders of development or to the aspirations of the communities involved, and in any event totally outside human control. Further, all of us have suffered from a lack of definition of the idea, so that there has been no common basis for discussion.

Some of the differences in the approach to the question of freedom can certainly be ascribed to another matter which also deeply affected the discussion of nationalism; that is, the evident relationship between each man's theoretical views and his area of study. Horton, Gallagher, Ibish, and Farmanfarmaian, for example, talked to each other in a kind of shorthand because they are all concerned with the Arab world. Gómez Millas and Silvert were compatible not only because of old acquaintance, but also because they wrangle with the same problem area. And so it went for all. Let us here note, then, that Bayne, Silvert, Gómez Millas, Gallagher, and Ibish were the most concerned with questions of mass participation, democratic procedures, decision-making, and the other elements of what can be synthesized as "freedom." The reason is almost certainly that they are all involved with the most politically national of all the countries treated—Italy, Japan, Argentina, Chile, Lebanon, Tunisia—where pragmatism, relativism, consensus, communications systems, and the like all are seen as having a crucial bearing on the capacity for continued development. On the other hand the most stylized theory designed for broadest application was advanced—not remarkably, if one reflects for a moment—by those dealing with the least articulated, the least complex societies.

Silvert ended by arguing that modernization can be a most threatening as well as rewarding process, involving as it does the rapid generation of power as the human community becomes more interwoven and interdependent, more capable of mass barbarism at the same time as greater individual freedom becomes possible. If, indeed, there is a positive relationship between freedom and continued development, then it is time to stop treating the subject of voluntaristic social organization with what W. G. Runciman in his *Social Science and Political Theory* calls the "ice cream fallacy"—you like vanilla, and I like chocolate, and that is all the weight we can give to a choice between leadership which consecrates continued authoritarianism, and leadership which prepares the way for ever-increasing areas of rational and effective choice.

On this hortatory note, Silvert thanked the participants for their enthusiasm, good nature, and imaginative contributions. In the names of the Messrs. Grondahl, Bayne, Gallagher, Horton, and Rusinow, as well as those of the absent associates of the AUFS, he expressed gratitude for the assistance given by the discussants.

With the blackboard bearing the multilingual goodbyes behind the chairman, and the fog of a North Italian spring pressing in from the windows, the conference adjourned.

Index

Index

The meeting at Villa Serbelloni, Bellagio, Italy, which provided the substance for *Discussion at Bellagio* was the first international conference under auspices of the American Universities Field Staff. Although the gathering itself was a new departure, it actually was an extension of AUFS work in comparative studies, a program activity in progress for several years.

Established as a nonprofit corporation in 1951 by a group of universities and colleges to undertake a continuing study of foreign societies, the American Universities Field Staff functions as an academic foreign service. Staff members spend extended periods of time in countries with which they are thoroughly familiar to report on significant developments. Periodically, they return to the United States, where they serve as visiting faculty on campuses of the sponsoring colleges and universities.

The institutions now associated with the AUFS program are the University of Alabama, Brown University, the California Institute of Technology, Carleton College, Dartmouth College, the Harvard University Graduate School of Business Administration, Indiana University, the University of Kansas, Michigan State University, Tulane University and the University of Wisconsin.

Books under the AUFS imprint include *A Select Bibliography: Asia, Africa, Eastern Europe, Latin America; Bung Karno's Indonesia* and *The Formation of Malaysia*, by Willard A. Hanna; *Dimensions of Japan*, by Lawrence Olson; and *Education and the Social Meaning of Development*, by K. H. Silvert and Frank Bonilla. *Expectant Peoples: Nationalism and Development*, staff-written under the editorship of K. H. Silvert is a publication of Random House, New York.

The AUFS Reports from abroad, published serially, are available by subscription. They reach a steadily growing list of subscribers among colleges, libraries, business firms, news organs, secondary schools, and individuals who have a professional or personal interest in keeping abreast of world developments. The Reports provide authoritative source material on political, economic, and social trends in Asia, Africa, Latin America, and (to a limited extent) Europe.

For details about the
AUFS Reports Service, and AUFS books
write to:
AMERICAN UNIVERSITIES FIELD STAFF, INC.
366 Madison Ave., New York, N.Y. 10017